Frangipani

A practical guide to growing frangipani at home

First published in Australia in 2008 by
Reed New Holland
an imprint of New Holland Publishers (Australia) Pty Ltd
Sydney • Auckland • London • Cape Town
1/66 Gibbes St Chatswood NSW 2067 Australia
218 Lake Road Northcote Auckland 0627 New Zealand
86 Edgware Road London W2 2EA United Kingdom
80 McKenzie Street Cape Town 8001 South Africa

10 9 8 7 6 5 4 3 2 1

National Library of Australia Cataloguing-in-Publication Data:

Author: Stowar, John.
Title: Frangipani / authors, John Stowar, Linda Ross.
ISBN: 9781877069550 (pbk.)
Notes: Bibliography.
Subjects: Plumeria.
Other Authors/Contributors:
             Ross, Linda K.
Dewey Number: 635.93393

Publisher: Fiona Schultz
Project Editor: Yani Silvana
Designer: Tania Gomes
Production: Liz Malcolm
Printer: SNP Leefung, China

Opposite: *Plumeria obtusa* is widely grown and appreciated throughout the
world—an icon of the tropics.

Dedication

We dedicate this book to our partners Anne Stowar, Daniel Wheatley and Phil Gray.
Their support, encouragement and ongoing patience enabled three frangipani tragics to plough on
even when the weather worked against us.

Contents

Introduction 11
Climate Change 13

Part I: History 18

1: Plant Origins, Species and a Little Botany 20
Origins 21
Name 22
The 'Tree of Riches' Story 23
Species 24

2: Dissemination 30
Asia 32
Hawai'i and the USA 33
Australia 36

Part II: Science 44

3: Appreciation and Characteristics 46
Growth Cycle 49
Plant Habit 49
Flower Shape 51
Flower Structure and Pollination 52
Fragrance 54
Colour 60
Texture 64
Leaf Shape 65

Part III: Growing 66

4: Care 68
Feeding 70
Transplanting Advanced Plants 71
Pots and Planters 74
Pruning 77

5: Troubleshooting 80
Overwintering in Cold Climates 80
Pests and Diseases 84

6: Propagation 94
Cuttings 94
Propagation by Seed 100
Grafting 104

7: Cultivars 108
'Celadine' 111
Moragne Hybrids 112
Jim Little Hybrids 116
Steven Prowse Collection 118
Future Frangipanis 120
Named Cultivars 122
What Variety Is That? 126

A beckoning seat beneath this 'Celadine' tree. Roma Street Gardens, Brisbane, Australia.

Part IV: Design 128

8: Use in Design.........................130
Welcome Home 134
Around the Home.............................136
Public Spaces..................................137
Water Gardens.................................138
Courtyards.......................................140
Lighting...142
Privacy Screens and Hedging...........143
Pools..145
Balconies and Terraces.....................148
Bonsai..151
By the Seaside..................................152
Frangipane Tart................................154

9: Tropical Garden Style 156
Fellowship of the Frangipani 160
Also Known as Frangipani................172

10: Significance..........................174
Temples, Public Parks and Historic Homes...175
Botanic Gardens and Collections....................180

11: Decoration and Art 184
Decorating with Frangipani..............186
Frangipanis in Art.............................193

Appendix: Specimens, Nurseries
and Gardens 196
Glossary...202
References and Further Reading.......208
Thank You..214
Gardens and Garden Designers 218
Photographers 222

Plumeria 'Capalaba Pink',
Tweed Heads, Australia.

Introduction

If you've picked up this book, odds are you enjoy frangipanis as much as we do. You might be wondering, though, how we managed to fill an entire book on them. Well, easy. Frangipanis are fragrant, fascinating, frivolous and foolproof. No other flowering tree comes in as many colours or fragrances, is as widely grown around the world, or means as much to as many different cultures. The frangipani has always been in vogue—who could tire of its simple perfection?

Frangipanis are synonymous with sunny holidays and the tropical garden style. People who live in colder climates would do anything to be able to grow one, while those who live in the tropics regard them as familiar. In India and South-East Asia, the intoxicating scent of frangipanis fills the grounds of many temples, while in Hawai'i their delicate flowers are strung together to make leis, the traditional welcoming wreaths. Everywhere it appears the frangipani is a symbol of a happy soul and friendly spirit.

These beautiful trees are also surprisingly resilient. Given a warm position, they can perform brilliantly in subtropical or even temperate regions, indeed, in all frost-free conditions. They are able to withstand exposure to salt-laden air and to flourish in the most inauspicious of situations—even in shallow soil on top of rock, they'll hold on tenaciously. With just a little bit of care, gardeners in frosty climates can grow frangipanis as indoor or conservatory plants, or you can expend a little more energy and lift them from the garden each year before frosts are likely to occur. No matter where you live, you can grow one, and here we'll show you how.

More than anything, though, this book is a celebration of the frangipani and its thousands of varieties. Although the majority is derived from one species, *Plumeria rubra*, many are unique in character—in their size, flower colour and shape, leaf shape, texture and perfume. They have different times

OPPOSITE: An Australian strain of frangipani commonly called 'Fruit Salad' for its mixed fruit salad colours and markings.

and durations of flowering, which means that you can always find one to suit your needs. But frangipanis can also be unpredictable, and that is another part of their charm. Growing frangipanis can bring you years of pleasure, and we want to inspire you to enjoy them as much as we do.

Just living is not enough! One must have sunshine,
freedom and a little flower.

Hans Christian Andersen

The frangipani provides shade, beauty and fragrance to the 'outdoor room' of the twenty-first century.

Climate Change

Is there a better tree for the challenges ahead than the frangipani? With global warming a fact, we can no longer squander water, even in regions where it has hitherto been plentiful. In many parts of the world, water requirements are starting to become the most important consideration in plant selection, and this is where frangipanis come into their own. With their fleshy leaves and stems, these trees are extraordinarily resilient to lack of moisture. Under relentless sun and heat—except for extremes—they not only survive, but bloom abundantly.

Frangipanis are also hardy in a number of other ways. In areas where fire is a recurrent threat, they are protected, like rainforest plants, by the high moisture content in both the stems and the leaves. In salt-laden atmospheres, and in urban areas where air pollution is detrimental to the health of so many species, deciduous frangipanis—along with other species tolerant of air pollution, like plane trees, ginkgoes and Tree of Heaven (*Ailanthus sp.)*—shed any accumulated gunk with the leaves. They are also resilient to weed invasion and pests, and so will continue to thrive as more gardeners reduce their use of chemical pesticides.

Nor is it likely that frangipanis will themselves become a pest. Too often in the past, introduced plant species have escaped from gardens and threaten native plants. This exacerbates the continuing loss of habitat due to urban development and the increasing demands of forestry, agriculture and mining. In all the ecological studies undertaken, of which we are aware, frangipanis have never been deemed to have significant weed potential.

As more of us move to cities and suburbs, gardens will diminish in size, and much will be asked of the few plants that can be accommodated. Compact species will be the choice of many gardeners, while others will benefit from large varieties that have the capacity to grow well in containers. Frangipanis can meet both these needs, and current research will inevitably lead to an increased range of smaller growing varieties. All frangipanis are suitable container plants.

In the latter part of the twentieth century the appreciation of nature and the desire for some form of garden, even in the most derelict backyard, is a direct result of the pressure and tension of modern living in overcrowded space. There is now a compulsive urge to get the fingers into the soil to receive that therapeutic healing of the senses, which the close contact with nature and growing things imparts.

Beatrice Bligh *Cherish the Earth—the Story of Gardening in Australia*

Gardens have become smaller, and a more important feature of the home—restful havens in which we can reconnect with the natural world and its rhythms. For people who live in frosty regions, seasonal cycles are clearly defined; but for those in tropical and warm-temperate climates, where most plants are evergreen, deciduous frangipanis are indicators of seasonal change. They are also ideal for time-strapped gardeners. Our lives today are filled with work, family, socialising and leisure pursuits, and this can leave little time for tending to plants. Frangipanis are the *ultimate* in low maintenance. If they do need to be pruned once in a while, they instantly provide cuttings to plant elsewhere or give to friends.

In researching this book, we were often struck by the number of people who, without any encouragement, unhesitatingly proclaimed frangipani was their favourite

flower. The historian Dr Dorothy Gibson-Wilde told us contentedly that she 'woke every morning to the scent of frangipani', and there is now abundant evidence of the power of such sensual experiences to contribute to our well-being. A return to nature can even mean a return to health. Research in the field of eco-psychology has revealed that hospital patients recover faster and with less medication when they simply have a view of plants.

Those who contemplate the beauty of the earth find reserves of strength that will endure as long as life lasts. There is symbolic as well as actual beauty in the migration of birds, the ebb and flow of tides, the folded bud ready for spring. There is something infinitely healing in the repeated refrains of nature—the assurance that dawn comes after the night and spring after the winter.

Rachel Carson, *Silent Spring*

There was an old, twisty frangipani tree in the backyard of the terrace house in Ashfield where we lived until just before I turned five. I couldn't make it up the corrugated iron ramp into the tree house in the tall turpentine tree where the big kids played, so the low slung branches of the frangipani were my favourite retreat. I loved the spicy scent of its flowers and the easy curve of the bough where I could sit. I'd heard the word 'drawing room' somewhere and naturally I thought it was a room where you drew. So I called the frangipani tree my drawing room and I would spend happy, sunlit hours etching...fairies and elves into its soft bark.

Geraldine Brooks, *author*

OPPOSITE: This frangipani is happy in a small raised bed that restricts its root system. The red-flowering shrub is *Magaskepasma erythrochlamys*, with bougainvillea and lavender, Freshwater, Sydney, Australia.

History

1. Plant Origins, Species and a Little Botany

Visitors to many parts of Asia often assume that frangipanis must be of Asian origin, such is the reverence for them in much of this region. When aged trees are encountered in large numbers around temples and the flowers themselves are favoured as offerings to Buddha, how could it be otherwise? In parts of India, the frangipani represents eternity because of its remarkable capacity to continue flowering well after a branch has been picked. However, records indicate that frangipanis were actually unknown in the East before the sixteenth century, when Portuguese and Spanish traders introduced the specimens they had collected from various parts of the New World and the Caribbean.

Frangipanis, which are native to the semi-deciduous forests of southern Mexico and Panama, were featured in The *Badianus Manuscripts* of 1552. According to this collection of Aztec herbal remedies, compiled during the early years of Spanish rule, the indigenous people used the frangipani for a wide range of medicinal purposes, from poultices to emetics. Soon the hardy shrub with beautiful fragrant flowers was a favourite of the Spanish, who planted it around their churches, monasteries and cemeteries, and took it with them as they explored the world.

Like numerous fruits and vegetables, many ornamental flowering plants of tropical America acclimatised so successfully in the Old World tropics that their geographic origins became masked. The sweetly fragrant frangipani (Plumeria rubra), a native of the West Indies, was widely planted in the East Indies and became known as the Pagoda Tree or Temple Flower, from its frequent plantings near Buddhist temples.

Richard Aitken, *Botanical Riches*

Origins

Thousands of years ago frangipanis were being cultivated in the area of present-day Mexico. In Aztec and Mayan civilisations, frangipani was known as Cacalo, Cacaloxochitl and Flor de Mayo. Mayans believed that the flower was created by K'akoch, the father of the gods, and it was intrinsically woven into their mythology. It was a sacred symbol of truth and immortality, and any commoner who picked or smelled its flowers could be punished with death. Medicinally it was used as a stimulant and restorative.

You can still find frangipanis growing in their native habitat today. It is common in Mexico in most dry forests below about 1500 metres (4900 feet), although in exceptional cases it does grow up to about 1800 metres (5900 feet). Plentiful examples can be found in the Tehuacan-Cuicatlan Valley of southern Puebla and northern Oaxaca, where it grows alongside the cactus *Cephalocereus columna-trajani*.

PREVIOUS PAGE: *Plumeria rubra* f. *lutea*.
BELOW: Sketch of *Plumeria* from 'Botanical Riches' by Richard Aitkens.
Sketch from 'Trees and Shrubs' manuscript albums British, c. 1802–04 Volume 1, details from folio 20.

Name

The name 'frangipani' is reputedly derived from the surname of an Italian aristocrat, Senior Frangipani, who created a perfume to scent gloves after the leather had been tanned. The native flowering trees of the Caribbean reminded early white settlers of this fragrance, and they named the trees accordingly—an enchanting and credible story. Another explanation suggests that French colonists in the region thought that the white latex produced by the trees resembled coagulated milk—in French this is termed *frangipanier*.

In some countries, including the United States, frangipanis are commonly known as plumeria, and this is also the scientific term shared by all the species within the frangipani group. The name was coined by a French botanist, Joseph Pitton de Tournefort, to honour fellow French botanist and missionary, Charles Plumier (1646–1704), who assisted Tournefort on plant-collecting expeditions. After his first successful trip, Plumier was appointed Royal Botanist by King Louis XIV, and became the most notable botanical explorer of the time. Plumier made three voyages to the Caribbean in 1689, 1693 and 1695, describing and sketching plants and animal life. His beautiful drawings are curated at the Natural History Museum, Paris.

Blossoms fell...glistening like golden coins from the Tree of Riches. Honolulu, Hawai'i.

The Tree of Riches—
A French and West Indian Legend

Legend has it that, before he set off around the world in search of riches, the botanist Charles Plumier consulted a fortune teller, who told him: 'Search for a tree that grows near churches and graveyards. Its blossoms are the colour of the new moon; its fragrance will overpower your soul. If you uproot it, the leaves and flowers continue to grow. When you find it you shall be rich.'

Plumier travelled far and wide until at last he reached the West Indies. Here he went to an old woman known for her wisdom and asked if she knew of a tree like the one that the fortune teller had described. The old woman told him that she did: 'You must go to the church near here, at midnight, on a full moon night. There you will see a tree spreading its branches along the wall. Shake the branches, and you will soon see riches beyond imagining.'

Plumier did as he was told. He found the tree and shook it. Blossoms fell all around him, glistening like golden coins. The fragrance did overcome his soul, and he suddenly realised what real riches were: the calm beauty of the night, the sweet scent of the flowers, the peace of the churchyard. He stopped looking for material wealth and instead continued to look for wealth in nature, discovering many plants. The tree that he found was named Plumeria *after him.*

Used with permission of author, A. Pellowski

Species

Frangipanis belong to the Family Apocynaceae, commonly called the Dogbane family, most of whose members contain the same distinctive milky white latex.

Members of the Apocynaceae Family

Acokanthera, Adenium, Allamanda, Alstonia, Alyxia, Apocynum, Carissa, Cascabella (syn. Thevetia), Catharanthus, Cerbera, Chonemorpha, Hoya, Mandevilla, Marsdenia, Nerium, Ochrosia, Pachypodium, Parsonsia, Tabernaemontana, Trachelospermum, Vinca and, of course, *Plumeria*.

Frangipani/*plumeria* nomenclature has long been confused, largely because of the differing approaches of plant taxonomists. The 'splitters', who maintain that the numerous observed forms warrant separate species status, have now been outnumbered by the 'lumpers', who hold the view that the observed diversity within their natural range merely reflects geographical variation within a handful of species.

Plumeria rubra f. rubra 'Donald Angus', Redland Bay, Queensland.

Plumeria rubra

All coloured varieties are believed to have *Plumeria rubra* in their ancestry, an understorey tree from the semi-deciduous tropical forests of Mexico to Panama. There are perhaps thousands of varieties, which usually grow as large deciduous shrubs or small trees to a height of 8 metres (26 feet) with a broadly rounded canopy, often greater in diameter than the height. They are traditionally divided into four groups according to the principal flower colour. *Plumeria rubra* f. *rubra*, sometimes called West Indian Red Jasmine, has pink-red blooms usually with a small yellow 'eye', as well as a significant perfume and good 'substance' (petal texture). *Plumeria rubra* f. *lutea* has large, fragrant yellow flowers, which fade to white with age and are sometimes lightly flushed pink on the underside. Their branches tend to droop then bend up again at the ends. *Plumeria rubra* f. *tricolor* has flowers that are predominantly white but have a yellow centre and rose pink outer margins. Their fragrance is varied and sometimes intense. *Plumeria rubra* var. *acutifolia*, the fourth group and most commonly grown tree, has white blooms with a yellow centre.

Plumeria rubra var. acutifolia

The most widely grown of all frangipanis throughout the world and the most common form in the wild is *Plumeria rubra* var. *acutifolia*. After several revisions of thinking, this is now considered to be the correct name for the plant that everyone knows as the frangipani. Its flowers are creamy white with a signature yellow centre—occasionally lightly flushed with pink, especially on the reverse—and has the unforgettable and widely acclaimed fragrance. This is the type often referred to in India and the Far East as the Pagoda Tree. In China it is called Egg Flower, and in Hawai'i and the islands of the Caribbean it is known as Common Yellow, Graveyard Flower and 'Celadine'. 'Celadine'—*Plumeria rubra* var. *acutifolia* 'Celadine'—is now the registered name in the list of cultivars held by the Plumeria Society of America, which is the international registration authority (see Cultivars on page 111) for the species and referred to hereafter as 'Celadine'.

Today cultivars of *Plumeria rubra* extend the colour range to apricots, salmons, orange, gold and even lavender, and the search continues for elusive new colours that will set the heart of frangipani enthusiasts racing.

Plumeria rubra var. *acutifolia*, also known as 'Celadine'.

Plumeria obtusa, Hawaii.

Plumeria alba at Nong Nooch Tropical Botanic Gardens, Thailand.

Plumeria obtusa

Originating in the Bahamas, Jamaica, Cuba, Puerto Rico, Hispaniola and British Honduras, *Plumeria obtusa* is an evergreen tree with shiny, dark green, leathery leaves, characteristically rounded at the apex. It has almost pure white, luminous and intensely fragrant flowers, which grow in large clusters. As the tree can be very variable in some characteristics, especially flower size, petal shape, and leaf size and shape, the numerous forms were once given separate species status—up to 40 are listed by the *Atlas of Florida Vascular Plants*. It has also hybridised, giving rise to further forms, increasing the confusion in nomenclature. The so-called Singapore frangipani and its cousins are of this parentage and regarded by many to have the best fragrance of all frangipanis. In cooler climates this species may become deciduous to varying degrees, which may also differ from one year to the next. Even within the tropics, where it flowers almost continuously, *Plumeria obtusa* may occasionally become briefly dormant. Some taxonomists regard *Plumeria sericifolia,* whose leaf undersides and petioles are covered with fine short hairs (pubescence), as simply a form of *P. obtusa.* Others classify a form of this species that originates on the island of Hispaniola as a distinct species, *Plumeria tuberculata*. It has rough protuberances on its trunk and narrow, glossy, strap-like leaves.

Plumeria alba

As the name suggests to those familiar with Latin, *Plumeria alba* has white flowers (with a small yellow centre). Known as the Nosegay Tree, this deciduous species, 2–9 metres (6–30 feet) tall, originates in Puerto Rico and the Virgin Islands, where it is now considered rare and endangered. Like *Plumeria obtusa,* it varies in characteristics depending on environmental factors. Its leaves are alternate, narrow, dark or light green, and glossy with blunt tips and recurved margins. They are also heavily indented with coarse lateral veins. The flowers' petals tend to be separated and recurved, and in strong sunlight they turn yellow. On picking they brown quickly. This species is considered the best source of essential oils for perfumes and toiletries due to its strong fragrance. In India it is grown extensively and used medicinally in Ayurvedic practice for deep cleansing, stress reduction and sleep disorders.

Plumeria cubensis

Coming from the Caribbean islands and Cuba, *Plumeria cubensis* is an evergreen tree which grows to 8 metres (26 feet) in height, with dark green, waxy leaves, which are somewhat twisted around the edges and densely whorled on the stems. Its yellow-centred white flowers are strongly fragrant. They are characterised by widely spaced, rounded and waxy petals, which are held in erect clusters on long peduncles.

Plumeria stenophylla
(syn. *P. filifolia*)

This evergreen shrub from the Dominican Republic and Cuba is of dwarf habit and has narrow lanceolate leaves. It bears clusters of yellow-centred white flowers which have narrow petals and are delicately fragrant. The seedlings of this species grow true to type, and in the wild this is an extremely tough species, found in cactus scrubland on sandy, poor alkaline soils. *Plumeria stenophylla nana* is a compact shrub variety, which grows to 2.5 metres (8 feet). It has narrow, dark, curly green foliage and masses of pure white flowers in summer, but unfortunately no scent.

TOP: *Plumeria cubensis,* at Mt Coot-tha Botanic Gardens, Queensland.

BOTTOM: *Plumeria stenophylla* growing in Mt Coot-tha Botanic Gardens, Queensland.

Plumeria pudica

Commonly called Bridal Bouquet, *Plumeria pudica* originates in Venezuela, Colombia and Panama. The upright and vigorous suckering habit of this evergreen shrub-like plant often results in a thicket, growing to 6 metres (20 feet). Its leaves are glossy and have a distinctive spoon shape, with pointed tips—some people describe it as 'fiddle-shaped'. Year-round it bears large clusters of blooms on the ends of its branches. Each flower is around 50 millimetres (2 inches) in diameter and bright white, with a tiny yellow centre. It has no fragrance during the day, but, according to some enthusiasts, releases a delicate scent at night. Pruning young plants of this variety encourages a desirable strongly branching habit. It is also resistant to plumeria rust.

Plumeria pudica growing in Fairchild Tropical Botanic Garden, Miami, USA.

Plumeria caracasana

Closely related to *Plumeria pudica,* this species comes from the Dominican Republic. Reaching 8 metres (26 feet) in height, it is often planted as a street tree in India. It has large and pendulous inflorescences with distinctive ammonia-like fragrance, and flowers with widely separated and strongly recurved petals. The smooth bark becomes shiny and bronze-like with age. Some botanists regard it as a form of *P. pudica*.

Plumeria caracasana at Nong Nooch Tropical Botanic Gardens, Thailand.

Medicinal Properties

The white latex of frangipani, instantly apparent upon wounding the trees, occurs in laticifers, fine tubes within the wood. Their living cells produce a complex mix of chemicals within the latex, which includes essential oils containing fragrant alcohols known as terpenes. The latex is believed to be the plant's natural mechanism to ward off predators and, while it is a skin irritant for some people and toxic in concentration, it has been used by the native Caribbean Indians as a poultice to treat skin inflammations of bacterial origin.

This use was recorded in the *Badianus Manuscripts*, which were compiled and translated into Latin by two Native Americans in 1552 in the Catholic College of Santa Cruz. Intended to fuse Aztec knowledge with European traditions, the illustrated collection lists more than 100 medical conditions with recommended herbal treatments.

Frangipani latex was recommended as an anti-rheumatic treatment and for ulcers, wounds and decayed teeth. Frangipani bark was listed as a purgative in the *Badianus Manuscripts*.

In 1895 *The American Journal of Pharmacy* again described the medicinal uses of frangipani bark, that from *Plumeria alba* being recommended for the treatment of herpes, syphilis and syphilitic ulcers, and bark from *Plumeria rubra* var. *acutifolia* for abscesses, gonorrhoea and fever.

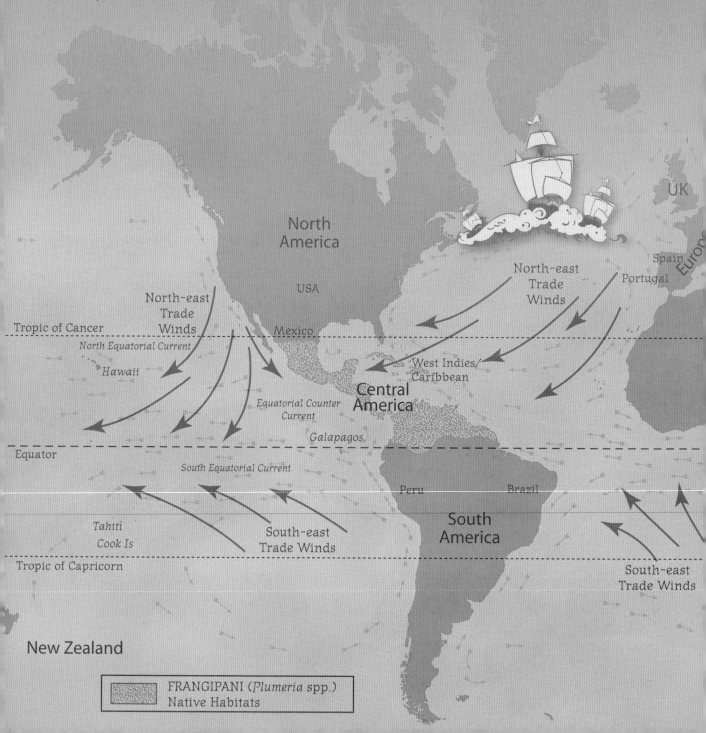

From the sixteenth century, galleons and smaller craft depended on ocean currents and trade winds to traverse the seas. Frangipanis were taken from the New World to the Old and ultimately spread to the world's tropical islands.

North America

UK

Spain

Portugal

Europe

USA

North-east Trade Winds

North-east Trade Winds

Tropic of Cancer

North Equatorial Current

Mexico

Hawaii

West Indies/ Caribbean

Central America

Equatorial Counter Current

Galapagos

Equator

South Equatorial Current

Peru

Brazil

South America

Tahiti

Cook Is

South-east Trade Winds

Tropic of Capricorn

South-east Trade Winds

New Zealand

FRANGIPANI (*Plumeria* spp.) Native Habitats

2. Dissemination

Sailing from Palos in Spain in 1492, Christopher Columbus pioneered the route to the New World. For years after his landing in the Caribbean, Columbus was convinced that he had actually landed in the Indies (the former name of southern and South-East Asia), which is why the area gained the name West Indies. By 1494 the island of Hispaniola was settled. Soon afterwards, in 1519, the Spaniard Hernán Cortés arrived in the area, to find the social strata of the local Aztec and Mayan civilisations signified by flowers.

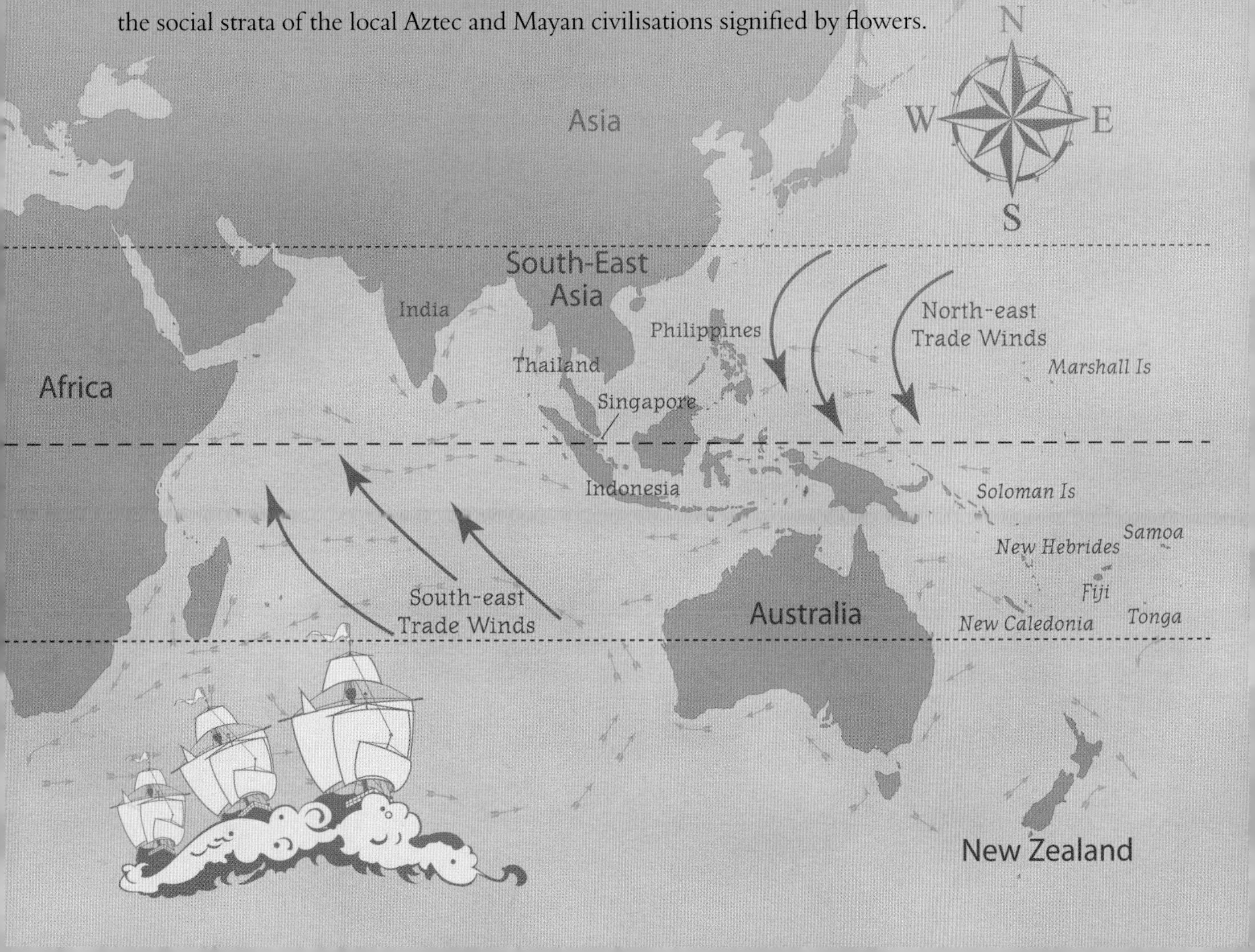

Asia

N
W E
S

South-East Asia

India

Philippines

North-east Trade Winds

Marshall Is

Africa

Thailand

Singapore

Indonesia

Soloman Is

Samoa

New Hebrides

South-east Trade Winds

Australia

Fiji

New Caledonia

Tonga

New Zealand

Under the command of Cortés, the conquistadors plundered the region, sending cargo back to Spain and its European customers that included avocados, tomatoes, vanilla and chocolate, as well as gold, silver, precious stones, pearls, salt, spices, tobacco, cotton, indigo and cochineal dyes, tortoiseshell and exotic timbers. Frangipanis could well have been part of their cargo, although they demonstrated little interest in plants unless they had an apparent financial reward, like tobacco.

Asia

Buoyed by the North Equatorial Current and buffeted by the Trade Winds, the conquistadors travelled to the Philippine Islands, discovered by Ferdinand Magellan for Spain in 1521. Then, from around 1530 onwards, the Portuguese, rivals of the Spanish who had settled in Brazil, started to connect the New World with the Old World tropics. The Portuguese established a trade route to the west coast of India, sailing south around Africa's Cape of Good Hope and brought chilli and cayenne, which became staple ingredients in Indian cooking. They also brought tropical fruits, such as pawpaw and pineapple, and it is highly likely that many of their galleons would have had stems of the captivating frangipani on board, resulting in the flower's immediate introduction into Asia.

Pink and red flowering frangipanis in the grounds of the Royal Palace, Bangkok, Thailand.

In 1653, when working for the Dutch East Indies Company, the Dutch naturalist George Eberhard Rumpf (1627–1702) found frangipanis growing in Ambon, in the Moluccan chain of eastern Indonesia. Although it seemed that the plants had been brought by the Portuguese, he included them in his *Herbarium Amboinensis,* a description of local plants published around 1747. To this day, frangipanis continue to be favoured trees for Indonesian Muslim cemetery planting.

In the East, Buddhists quickly adopted the frangipani as their Temple Flower, and both Buddhist monks and Catholic clergy would plant them around temples, monasteries and churches as they spread their respective religions throughout the Asian region. Many gnarled and aged specimens can still be seen around such buildings today, particularly in the Philippines and Thailand, where Catholicism was accepted early. The flower is perhaps less prevalent in China and Vietnam, where Catholics were reportedly persecuted and white-flowering, fragrant frangipanis were deemed to be the abode of ghostly spirits. However, it is recorded that in 1793 frangipani plants were available in Chinese nurseries and favoured for cemetery-planting, because of their capacity to thrive without attention. The appearance of fallen flowers on the grave was also considered a subtle reminder to the living to pay a visit.

In Thailand and India today there is considerable research into frangipanis. This has extended people's appreciation of the tree beyond its traditional cemetery associations, and the frangipani force is now strong in both countries. Enthusiasts have set their sights on developing the elusive blue frangipani. Expensive Lilac varieties from breeders in Thailand and India are available, but they will become cheaper as nurseries get larger numbers.

Thousands of varieties are being bred in these countries to satisfy the voracious appetite for new colours and styles in the West. While researching this book, we found interesting new varieties available online for up to US $330 each cutting.

Hawai'i and the USA

When tourism took off in the twentieth century, frangipanis were quickly adopted as symbols of a relaxed tropical lifestyle, and Hawai'i became the epicentre for frangipani adoration.

The first frangipani in Hawai'i has been attributed to Dr Wilhelm

Hillebrand, who lived in Hawai'i from 1851–71. German botanist and chief physician at Queens Hospital, Honolulu, he returned with a 'Celadine' plant—commonly called a Yellow—from a trip to Asia in 1860. A cutting reputed to be from the original tree led to the specimen that can be seen now at the Foster Botanical Garden in Honolulu, which Dr Hillebrand founded.

As in Asia, Hawai'ian locals soon came to know the frangipani as the Graveyard Flower. Over the years numerous forms of 'Celadine' appeared on the islands, and those with especially yellow centres gained the name Common Yellow. However, it wasn't until the 1940s, when tourists started to visit the area, that it became appreciated for its suitability as a lei flower (see Decoration on page 184).

The first red is thought to have arrived here at the turn of the century from Mexico, either via Mrs Paul Neumann, wife of a German consul stationed in Honolulu, or a Mr Gifford, landscaper for the Royal Hawaiian Hotel, Oahu, Hawai'i. This is an important introduction, as the red, through natural hybridisation and breeding, has led to the incredible variety of colours and shapes in Hawai'i today.

Frangipani trees have been given countless common names. Most are of local significance, so this can cause confusion when that variety is then taken abroad.

Contrasting with a lush breadfruit tree, lichen-covered frangipanis are part of the mountainous landscape, Limahuli Botanic Gardens, Kaua'i, Hawai'i.

The white 'Singapore'—a form of *Plumeria obtusa*—was, in fact, named in Hawai'i. Mr Harold Lyon, a director of a sugar cane research station, planted the first specimen here in 1931, which he had obtained from a collection at the Singapore Botanic Gardens (established in 1913). To add to the confusion, the fact remains that frangipanis would have originally come from the Caribbean (see above).

There are now extensive collections of plumeria at the University of Hawai'i and at other sites in the island chain. A Mecca for frangi enthusiasts is Koko Crater Botanical Garden, on the island of Oahu. Here the focus is on drought-tolerant species, with a collection of around 60 mature trees as well as countless seedlings growing naturally beneath them. Planted in the crater of the volcano, the collection is particularly impressive when in full flower. Some of its trees have a canopy spread of up to 10 metres (33 feet), and they are planted at

approximately 5-metre (16-foot) centres. Walk up the sides of the crater for the best view over the collection—the trees form one continuous canopy when viewed from above.

The Dean Conklin Plumeria Grove was dedicated in 1977, to recognise the contribution to horticulture in Hawai'i of this plumeria enthusiast and member of the Board of Directors for the Friends of Foster Botanical Garden.

Venerable and draped with Spanish Moss, orchids and other bromeliads, this tree in the Foster Botanic Gardens is reputed to be the progeny of the original 'Celadine', Oahu, Hawai'i.

It was on Kauai in the Hawaiian islands, in the 1950s, that Mr William Moragne snr, after almost 20 years of experimentation, documented the first controlled hybridisations of the frangipani. They and their progeny remain some of our firm favourites among the cultivars (see Cultivars on page 110). Enthusiasts, nurserymen and staff at the University of Hawai'i continue to do research to this day.

Following on from the success of the species and cultivars in Hawaii, many American tourists fall in love with the flower and want to take them home. Today there are stands of bagged frangipani cuttings at airports ready for tourists to take back home as a memento of their holiday. Goodness knows how many of these small 20-centimetre (8-inch) cuttings actually make it home alive and strike!

Although Americans favour Hawaiian cultivars, plumerias are becoming the number one flower, with imports from Thailand, India and Australia feeding the hunger for new varieties. The Plumeria Society of America started in 1979 and membership now exceeds 3000. Florida, Texas and California are the primary growing states, but plumeria popularity is expanding to areas where its cultivation is less than ideal. Overwintering is de rigeur in these climates.

Australia

The vast, dry country of Australia has been worn down over millennia. In most parts, weathering has resulted in exceptionally nutrient-poor soils, upon which have developed a remarkably diverse and captivating flora. Although the nomadic Aborigines have managed to survive off this land for perhaps 50,000 years, the first European settlers, arriving in 1788, made food production their priority. The new arrivals found no familiar food growing naturally, and their journals, ships' logs and letters refer principally to the need for suitable plants for food, medicines and construction.

Over long and hazardous sea journeys from England—the journey took about nine months, via either South Africa's Cape of Good Hope or Rio de Janeiro in South America—suitable plants were progressively introduced. But the settlers also longed for ornamental plants that were familiar to them. As most settlers came from England, frangipani was not yet a plant they knew, but it is recorded that when the first primrose arrived, it caused a stampede at the wharf.

Arriving in 1826, Australia's first nurseryman/landscape designer, Thomas Shepherd, encouraged by the Governor, set out to produce plants commercially from the Government gardens. (These gardens had been established in 1816 and became Sydney's Royal Botanic Gardens.) However, this was an unprofitable venture, so he encouraged the wealthier settlers to design their new estates according to the style with which he was familiar in England, that of landscape designer Humphrey Repton.

Shepherd prepared a series of seven lectures on *Landscape Gardening*, and presented the first lecture in 1835 but, unfortunately, died before he could

OPPOSITE: 'Celadine' is synonymous with Sydney, Australia.

BELOW: Flagged with Sydney sandstone, this welcoming entrance is shaded by a graceful tricoloured frangipani, perfect in scale to its setting.

deliver the series. His prepared text, however, survives. In this he extols the glories of the garden established by Alexander Macleay, the Colonial Secretary, at Elizabeth Bay House on the shores of Sydney Harbour:

From the first commencement, Mr Macleay has never suffered a tree of any kind to be destroyed until he saw the necessity of doing so. He thus retained the advantage of embellishment from his native trees and harmonised them with the foreign trees now growing … His botanic, flower, landscape, fruit and kitchen gardens are all on the first scale, and he has also expended large sums in digging out rocks, filling up hollows, making approaches and walks, grass flats, basins etc … and in the purchase of foreign trees and plants which have been arranged with great skill and taste … Ornamental lawns and polished shrubberies [are] furnished with choice trees and plants from England, China, Mauritius, the East Indies, North and South America, and from Moreton Bay, Norfolk Island, the Cape of Good Hope and other places. In a few years therefore, the beauties of Elizabeth Bay will be unrivalled.

While this was achieved and the garden's reputation spread far and wide, barely a fragment remains of its many magnificent acres. However, we do have records of the plants purchased, and they include frangipanis. In his own handwriting Macleay prepared a 'List of Plants Received at Elizabeth Bay—1836–43'. Received in May 1839 from Dr Nathaniel Wallich, Superintendent of the Calcutta Botanic Gardens, was *Plumeria acuminata* (an earlier name for *Plumeria rubra*). In his notebook, Macleay also lists seeds received between 1836–53, including item 151—*Plumeria hybrida* from England in August 1839. These are believed to be the earliest references to frangipanis in Australia.

Australia's settlement coincided, in the late eighteenth and early nineteenth centuries, with the great period of world plant collecting, and this ensured that gardens earned prime places in the new colony. As both an explorer and a botanist, Allan Cunningham contributed significantly to the colony's agricultural and horticultural development at both the Royal Botanic Gardens in Sydney, New South Wales, and the Experimental Gardens in Brisbane, Queensland. The Brisbane gardens were started in 1828 and displayed tropical plants, which were mostly unsuited to the cooler climates of the other major Australian State capitals. One of its stated roles was the acclimatisation of species collected from around the world, but coming to grips with the climatic diversity and vagaries of Australia's various settlements proved difficult. In the 1840s New South Wales was gripped by extreme drought and, perhaps because this was so foreign to someone from England, Alexander Macleay had to bring a gardener from Rio de Janeiro to oversee the development of the grounds at Elizabeth Bay House. Economic depression followed this drought, but the economy bounced back with the gold rushes of the 1850s. By the 1870s and '80s, the economy was again booming, culminating in the High Victorian style of architecture and garden design.

Blending the old and the now, two frangipanis flank either side of the central path, providing a lively backdrop to a contemporary planting.

Where the climate permitted, country mansions, city terrace houses and humble working men's cottages were all able to accommodate frangipanis. Sydney was found to be climatically very suitable for *Plumeria rubra* 'Acutifolia', and to this day inner-city gardens display this frangipani almost as a signature, with many trees reaching peak flowering around Christmas.

In 1862 Queensland's Acclimatisation Society established a garden at Bowen Park, near Brisbane Hospital, which occupied 18 hectares (45 acres), including a creek valley. In 1862 Alexander McPherson was appointed its park keeper, and in 1876 Bowen Park held an exhibition to promote the society's aim—to introduce, propagate and distribute useful plants from overseas countries. In 1885 the colonial botanist Frederick M. Bailey published the *Catalogue of Plants in the Two Metropolitan Gardens* (that is, Brisbane Botanic Gardens and Bowen Park). This included a listing for '*Plumeria acuminata*—known as Franchipanier/Pagoda Tree from East India'.

Baron Sir Ferdinand Von Mueller arrived in Adelaide in 1847 and became Government Botanist of Victoria in 1853. Keenly interested in the acclimatisation of both plants and animals, he travelled widely, published many scientific papers, was director of the Melbourne Botanic Garden from 1857–73, and fostered many other gardens and collections around Australia. Von Mueller also appointed Edwin Jephcott to establish the Brisbane Botanic Gardens. In 1864 Jephcott took up land in southern New South Wales, where he trialled exotic trees, from seeds provided by Von Mueller, prior to their planting at the Melbourne Botanic Garden.

Another key associate of Von Mueller was Eugene Fitzalan (1830–1911), horticulturist, nurseryman and botanical collector. Fitzalan arrived from England with his plant collection in 1849 and settled in Victoria. He moved to Brisbane in 1859, where he opened a seed and plant shop. On one of his plant-collecting travels, he visited Mexico, where it is likely that he collected frangipani samples, although there are no known

Not costing a cent, frangipanis grew easily from cuttings, appealing to inner-city working-class communities and surviving today as signature plants of these suburbs. Sydney, Australia.

records of his plants. Fitzalan corresponded with Von Mueller, who held him in high esteem. He also collected seed of indigenous species for Von Mueller.

Heading north from Brisbane, Bowen was established as a shipping port in 1861. Although a sprawling city today, its oldest parts contain many frangipanis surviving from the town's earliest days. At Bowen cemetery there is a large, well-established grove of *Plumeria obtusa* of various forms. At Muller's Lagoon in Davidson Park, near the centre of town, the Bowen Shire Council has planted recently a grove of around 60 trees, mostly *Plumeria rubra* in a range of colours and forms. The trees promise to make an eye-catching display in years to come.

Townsville, Australia's largest tropical city, was founded in 1864 and the Queens Gardens, its first botanic gardens, were begun in 1870. Unfortunately records are not available to substantiate the ages of specific early plantings here, but many old trees survive. According to the current curator, Chris Cole, an aged and propped *Plumeria rubra* 'Acutifolia' in Queens Gardens is estimated to be 80 to 90 years old.

Around the same time as Queens Gardens were being planted, nearby Magnetic Island was established as a weekend retreat for Townsville residents. Trees were brought to the island by the Armand family, who lived in Arcadia, and these included poincianas, tamarinds and frangipanis, which thrive to this day without any supplementary watering. While the native kapok tree, *Cochlospermum gillivraei*, is the official floral emblem for Townsville and Magnetic Island, it is the frangipani that features as the de facto floral symbol on much of the tourist literature and commercial signage.

Love Lane in the Townsville suburb of Mundingburra is a long street, planted for much of its length with frangipanis. Time has taken its toll, but it is a significant planting. Mr Tom Wyatt who was the council parks' foreman at the time the trees were introduced, in the late 1960s, related that cuttings were collected from Queens Gardens and private properties, and that the plants were propagated at the council nursery in 4-gallon (15-litre) paint tins and sanitary pans. The spacing of the trees along the street is variable, as is their size and age. This can be explained by the fact that residents—in true old Queensland style—initially objected to having a tree planted outside their property, but changed their minds as soon as they saw the frangipanis in flower.

Heat, Frost and Rain

The tolerance of frangipanis to extreme drought and prolonged torrential rain is clearly appreciated from assessment of rainfall figures for Townsville. Falling within the so-called 'dry tropics', plants in this region have to withstand not only extreme summer heat, but also extensive dry periods and soaking rain. Over the last decade, annual rainfall has averaged 1129 millimetres (44 inches). Of this only 125 millimetres (5 inches) was recorded for the usual dry period May–October.

As stated in the introduction, frangipanis are frost sensitive, but for reasons not yet fully understood, when a plant experiences clear skies and abundant sunshine, especially in winter, a measure of frost hardiness is imparted. Indeed, under those conditions, plants can sometimes tolerate frosts that would normally kill them. For example, in Alice Springs, central Australia, where frosts to minus 4 degrees Celsius are experienced for perhaps 40 days per year, frangipanis thrive.

In sunny western New South Wales, frosts are common to usually minus 2.5°C (31.3°F), but frangipanis are garden favourites in Broken Hill and Moree, along with Jacaranda, citrus, bauhinia and Silky Oak (*Grevillea robusta*). All are frost tender in places along the east coast of southern Australia, where winter days are often cloudy, with only one or two degrees of frost on rare occasions and frangipanis will survive only in the most sheltered of spots. Under more extreme cold, their culture outdoors in winter is not possible. However, enthusiasts in North America and northern China, among other places, have long circumvented this limitation. Even large specimens are sometimes dug and brought indoors to heated conservatories, garages and basements to overwinter.

What's in a Name?

Around the world the frangipani is known by many other names:

Plumeria (USA)

Frangipani (Australia and Caribbean)

Jasmine de Cayenne (Brazil)

Pagoda Tree, Temple Tree or White Champa (India)

Egg Flower (southern China)

Amapola (Venezuela)

Dok Champa or Champa Flower (Laos)

Waringin or Jepun (Bali)

Leelawadee or Lanthom (Thailand)

Bunga Kubur or Kemboja Kuning (Malaysia)

Lei flower, Pua Melia, Pumeli or Melia (Hawaii)

West Indian Jasmine (West Indies and the documents of early settlers and travellers)

Flor de Mayo (Mexico and El Salvador)

Flor de la Cruz (Guatemala)

Graveyard Tree (Caribbean Islands)

Sacuanjoche (Nicaragua's national flower)

Tipanier (Tahiti)

Pansal Mal, Temple Flower (Sri Lanka)

Aleli (Puerto Rico)

Cacalo (Ancient Mexico)

Nikti (Mayan)

Lirio Rojo (Cuba)

Cacaloxochitl (Ancient Mexico)

Frangipanier (France)

Cacalojoche (Costa Rica)

Pomelia (Sicily)

Unknown cultivar, Thirroul, Australia.

Science

3. Appreciation and Characteristics

*Beautiful when in flower and rather wonderful in winter, too,
bare of branch and somewhat Jurassic, its strange, dense form,
like clusters of long liverwurst sausages.*

Leo Schofield, *A Flurry of Frangipanis*

While some frangipani species are evergreen, in tropical and warm-temperate climates most trees are deciduous for one to three months of the year, losing their leaves either in winter or in periods of extreme dryness or wetness. The enthusiast sees beauty and architectural charm in the deciduous condition, but we have to acknowledge that others who have not yet succumbed to 'the fever' may see an awkward and ungainly branch structure which verges on the 'grotesque'. Some gardeners from cold climates unfamiliar with the genus have even believed deciduous plants to be dead.

All species have a spiral, alternate leaf arrangement, restricted to the ends of the otherwise bare branches, with the flowers appearing at the branch tips. While some will have only a single flowering each year in summer, many will flower sporadically from spring until the following winter with a succession of flushes. In tropical areas the sight of flowers at the ends of bare branches is part of the frangipani's appeal. In temperate climates, flowers tend to appear later in the season when the tree is in leaf. Flowering is strongly influenced by the amount of solar radiation that the tree receives during the previous autumn to ripen the branch tips, and the timing of flowering is determined

by microclimate. Trees separated by just a few metres may flower at different times. While each flower lasts for only a few days once fully open, the progressive opening of a cluster (technically, an umbellate cyme) may span months, with trees in tropical regions flowering much of the year—some individual trees produce upwards of 20,000 flowers in a year. Each flower has a tubulate base, which can be up to 15 millimetres (0.5 inches) long, on a pedicel (stalk) of around 20 millimetres (0.75 inches). The flowers are folded spirally when in bud and usually open with five waxy petals, occasionally more. The flowers vary in 'substance' from one variety to the next, and this influences their longevity and, in turn, their suitability for various uses.

PREVIOUS PAGE: A tricolour growing in Manly Vale, Australia.
ABOVE: In tropical Hawai'i, flowering tends to start on bare branches prior to leaf growth. Foster Botanic Gardens, Honolulu, Hawai'i.
RIGHT: Flower buds are twirled spirally with five waxy petals (although flowers with 4, 6 or 7 petals have been observed).

Growth Cycle

The frangipani's annual growth cycle has evolved to include a dormant period coinciding with months of drought in the arid tropical regions of Central America, Mexico and the Caribbean Islands. As autumn approaches, less sun, cooler temperatures and less moisture e.g. rain and dew, together contribute to the plant entering this dormant period. At this stage the leaves yellow, then drop, and flowering will stop. Dormancy is achieved when the coldest temperatures are reached and conditions are dry. (In areas of winter warmth and rain, frangipanis tend to be troubled with fungal diseases, as their roots are unable to dry out completely.)

This corresponds to the Northern Hemisphere winter season. Most varieties will lose their leaves and no care is required.

As temperatures increase during spring, plants break their dormancy and start to produce an inflorescence on their tips. Many will be in full flower before spring rains arrive and some trees, particularly those in tropical areas, will flower before producing leaves.

Active growth then occurs after the spring rains, as long as temperatures are warm; leaf growth is dominant at this time. The root systems regenerate, and stems will elongate. Many varieties will also continue to bloom and create new inflorescences. Some varieties, especially in tropical and subtropical areas, will set fruit at this time.

Plant Habit

Frangipanis generally have a balanced appearance, but there are always exceptions to the rule.

People often overlook the fact that individual plants within any species may vary widely in habit (that is, plant shape and branch structure), due to environmental factors, cultural conditions and genetics. Where frangipanis stretch to find the sun, they will be long and lanky in appearance, while other frangipanis in full sun will tend to be more compact. In frangipanis, genetics confers habits ranging from dense and compact, because of regular branching, to open and lanky, where stems are elongated rather than branched. For example, members of the 'Lutea' group of *Plumeria rubra* commonly possess the habit whereby branches droop

OPPOSITE: Without any intervention, trees in full sun tend to develop a compact umbrella shape. Sydney, Australia.

then bend up again at the ends, creating a pendulous weeping habit.

The habit of your plant will largely determine its suitability for various garden and landscape situations. Unfortunately, plant labels rarely refer to a tree's habit, and it is usually only after growing the variety that you learn its habit, especially under the prevailing conditions. Consult local botanic gardens and private collections as an indication of potential.

Top: In their dormant state the true character or 'habit' of the branch arrangement is revealed. Eventually the limbs of aged 'lanky' trees will bend and touch the ground. Koko Crater, Oahu, Hawai'i.

Left: Dwarf compact frangipanis like this Thai hybrid 'Pink 100' syn. 'Dwarf Watermelon' are highly prized specimans for pot culture. Chattachuk markets, Bangkok, Thailand.

Flower Shape

The flared, tubular shape and elegant simplicity of frangipani flowers are attractive enough in themselves, before you even consider their appealing waxy, pearly texture, their characteristic fragrance and their range of enchanting colours. Contributing to its simplicity of form is the fact that the reproductive flower parts—the stigma and style, and stamens and anthers—are hidden deep within the floral tube. All we can readily see is the floral tube and its lobes, or petals.

Frangipani flowers usually have five petals, although some surprise with four, others six, seven or more. Occasional flowers will have more or fewer petals, while on some extensively hybridised plants a significant proportion of blooms may have more petals than usual.

At bud stage the lobes are distinctively twisted (convolute), and this characteristic continues, to varying degrees, in the fully opened flower. In some varieties the lobes never fully open, and such a flower is referred to as having a 'shell', 'semi-shell' or 'tulip' form. In some cases flowers have distinctive variations, like the cultivar 'Madame Poni', which has a 'whirligig' shape, with pinched petals like small propellers (see Cultivars on page 110).

The lobes may be wide and rounded or narrow at the corolla tube, then rounded (obovate), elliptical or narrow. Occasionally varieties are found with

TOP LEFT: 'Theresa Wilder' has widely spaced narrow petals.
TOP CENTRE: 'Kuaka Wilder' has pointed, elliptical petals.
TOP RIGHT: 'Sharna's Rose' has full, rounded overlapping petals.
BELOW LEFT: 'Bali Whirl' is the world's only double frangipani bloom, with ten petals instead of the usual five.
BELOW CENTRE: 'Katie Moragne' has round reflexed petals that overlap with a distinctive notch.
BELOW RIGHT: 'Fruit Salad' has reflexed wide petals.

spoon-shaped (spatulate) petals. Spacing can vary widely, and there are differing degrees of overlapping (imbrication) with each lobe shape. Petal tips are either rounded or pointed. The petals may also be twisted or reflexed. The flower stalk (pedicel) is variously coloured from green to red and combinations in between. All of these characteristics are significant when considering varieties for registration as cultivars with the International Registration Authority.

Flowers that are larger than normal do seem to attract attention—and hybridists of all plants seem to place high value upon this—but, as with all frangipani characteristics, flower size is elusive. It is strongly influenced by growing conditions, the maturity of the plant itself and the time of flower production in the growing cycle. Flowers produced early in the growing cycle tend to be larger, while those at the end of the season can be much smaller than those usually seen on the particular variety. For the same reasons the number of flowers within an inflorescence is similarly very variable. And, as you might expect, selectors and hybridists place a high value on cultivars with 'knock-out inflos' (inflorescences).

Flower Structure and Pollination

A prime example of elusiveness in frangipanis relates to pollination. In most simple flowers there is an easy transfer of pollen grains from the stamens to the sticky stigma, either within the same flower (self-pollination) or from a separate flower (crosspollination). In frangipanis you would expect self-pollination; due to the flower structure, pollen can fall easily and directly onto the stigma, assisted perhaps by buffeting winds. However, because frangipani fruit set is commonly very low, relative to the number of blooms, it has been suggested that frangipanis are self-incompatible.

For many plant species bees and flies are common agents of pollination, but in frangipanis both the stamens and stigma are deeply positioned in the narrow floral tube, well out of reach of these insects. In the tree's Caribbean home, this does not seem to be a problem, as hummingbirds have evolved alongside the frangipani, with long, curved bills and long tongues which can reach deep within the floral tube—ideal for pollination. Attracted to colourful flowers—especially those with UV reflectance—hummingbirds are regular daytime visitors to the frangipani, coming in search of sugary nectar to meet their high energy requirements. In the course of their searching, they are recorded as unwitting pollinators, as are long-proboscis butterflies, but both are deceived because frangipanis are actually devoid of nectar.

White-and-cream-flowered frangipanis are highly visible at night and usually fragrant. This is when they receive other visitors, such as sphinx moths, which are attracted by seductive fragrances, either of apparent nectar sources or mimicked pheromones (the odours released by female moths when they are ready to mate). These moths earned their name due to the fact that their resting caterpillar stage resembles the Sphinx. They are also known as Hawk moths, because of the speed at which they fly. They can detect odour plumes from flowers reputedly up to 10 kilometres (6 miles) away. The sphinx moth has a long, curled proboscis and can reach deep into the flower in its futile search. In the process, pollen grains adhere to the moth's scaly body, enabling pollen to be transferred to the next flower. But the moths must be doubly disappointed—no female and no nectar. This is a prime example of pollination by deceit.

Sphinx moths are not stupid, and they soon learn that the search in frangipanis is futile. This may account for the fact that fruit production in most trees is very low. William A. Haber, during approximately 40 hours of day and night observation of frangipani flowers in Costa Rica, observed not a single sphinx moth. The study concluded that the moths actually learned to avoid frangipanis and to concentrate on those species that yielded nectar.

However, some sphinx moths have another reason to visit the frangipani. In spite of the fact that frangipani latex is toxic to most animals and insects, the Tetrio Sphinx Moth from Central America, Mexico and the West Indies is able to lay its eggs on frangipanis, and its larval caterpillars devour the

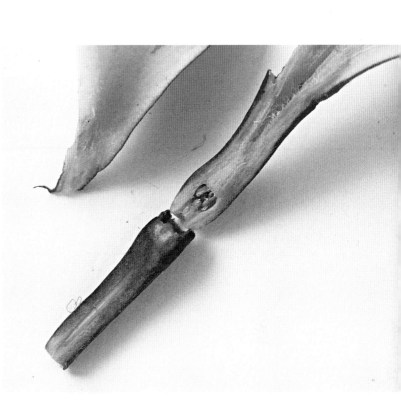

This dissected flower clearly reveals the deeply imbedded reproductive organs.

Germinating seeds under the ideal conditions after rain at the Koko Crater Botanical Garden, Oahu, Hawai'i.

foliage as their favoured food. This causes the long, velvety, deep blue-and cream-banded caterpillars to become unpalatable to potential predators, protecting them as they complete their metamorphoses into adult moths.

Of the numerous species of sphinx moths found worldwide, one that is also known as the Vine Hawk oth is perhaps the chief pollinator. However, in some parts of the world, thrips and ants have been observed as the most common flower visitors; they may indeed be the principal pollinators in some regions.

Where pollination and fertilisation is successful, fruits containing seeds develop. Usually paired in bean-like, tapered pods, they can be green or reddish and take about nine months to mature, at which point they split open and shed their seed. The tendency to fruit and set seed differs widely from one variety to another and from year to year—some varieties appear never to set seed.

Where conditions are suitable—for example, in a tropical climate with well-drained soil and collected moisture, say, in a rock crevice—self-sown seedlings are likely to appear. This is undoubtedly the reason for the countless forms of frangipani that have evolved over millennia. Some of these that remain true to type have been named as cultivars. But most seedlings of frangipanis that have been labelled as particular cultivars by some nurseries, have not been validly named, for the reasons that will become apparent later in the book.

Fragrance

A rose is a rose is a rose; but how disappointing when it doesn't have fragrance! Rarely is that the case with frangipanis. For many enthusiasts, fragrance is arguably the flower's most endearing feature—a combination of certainty and enchantment. Senior Frangipani had a hit with his fragrance, probably in the sixteenth century, but the plant itself sealed the popularity of the fragrance forevermore.

Oil glands within flowers contain essential oils, which by their very nature are volatile, with a complex chemical composition. Fragrant alcohols, known as terpenes, largely determine the particular nature of the fragrance—some argue that nothing can compare with that of the frangipani. Those who believe this, usually refer to *Plumeria alba, Plumeria obtusa* or *Plumeria rubra* var. *acutifolia* in which fragrance is consistent from one plant to the next.

One breath of her perfume and your city is lost.
Another, and you forfeit a kingdom.
 Ancient Japanese poet

A huge industry has developed around it, but today perfume is often of synthetic origin, after chemists in the 1920s were able to isolate the composition of flower fragrances using spectroscopic analysis. Perfume for the cosmetics and aromatherapy industries is now largely manufactured from aldehydes, organic compounds created in the laboratory, but a certain proportion relies on extracts from the natural essential oil, which is both fragrant and volatile.

India has long been the home of cultivation of *Plumeria alba*, where it is called White Champa, and this variety is said to yield the best quality oil, the 'queen of essential oils'. The incomparable Mrs M. Grieve refers to it in her *Modern Herbal* as 'the eternal perfume'. Reputed to foster a feeling of peacefulness and harmony, with a sweet, floral, 'green' aroma, the perfume is also said to be an aphrodisiac, but like many essential oils must be used 'with discretion'. Undiluted it can irritate the skin, and repeated contact of the pure 'absolute oil' may cause allergic dermatitis, so the usual custom is to dilute the essential oil (to a 2 to 5 per cent solution) with a carrier oil such as olive, jojoba or almond. It should be stored in a cool place away from ultraviolet (UV) light; amber glass bottles with tight-fitting lids are recommended. *Plumeria rubra* var. *acutifolia* is also harvested for its essential oil, though this is often said to be inferior to that of *Plumeria alba*.

Naturally, processing using traditional techniques of extraction produces a

very expensive product. Steam distillation or cold enfleurage, which involves absorption by a fatty substance like olive oil or purified lard, produce only small yields from a vast number of flowers. This is reflected in the pricing of the various categories of oil: the best is sold as 'frangipani absolute'.

The variety of aromas produced by the frangipani is demonstrated in the list on this page, and to this list can be added many other olfactory sensations depending on the beholder. In researching this book at a frangipani nursery in Australia, we unanimously agreed that one cultivar, 'Theresa Wilder', smelled distinctly like nasturtium, while 'coconut-like' and 'soapy' are common terms used by enthusiasts for other cultivars.

White-flowered frangipanis are most fragrant at night when pollinators are at large.

The Feast of Frangipani Fragrances

Those who smell a selection of the numerous varieties of *Plumeria rubra* are usually intoxicated with the feast of different fragrances. The descriptions from registered cultivars are determined by consensus from a number of people. Fragrances have been described as:

Sweet	carnation	Medium jasmine
Slight sweet	Faint rose	Strong jasmine
Mild sweet	Mild rose	Medium lavender
Strong sweet	Strong rose	Strong honeysuckle
Faint scent	Sweet rose-like	Strong citrus
Sweet fruity	Lemon	Raspberry
Strong fruity	Faint lemon	Strong sweet pea
Slight spicy	Strong lemon	Gardenia
Spicy	Faint peach	Narcissus
Faint spicy	Strong peach	

In 1991 at the University of Hawai'i, a team of Japanese researchers collected almost 500 grams (1 pound) of flowers from each of the cultivars 'Irma Bryan' and 'Celadine,' then subjected them to steam distillation. They produced a miniscule 70 milligrams (0.002 ounces) of essential oils. This was then analysed by mass spectrometry and gas chromatography, to reveal that each cultivar had its unique oil composition (12 hydrocarbons, 21 alcohols, 13 esters, 8 aldehydes and 20 other miscellaneous compounds were detected), with the composition of the yellow 'Celadine' being very different to that of the red 'Irma Bryan'.

As flower colours can vary within plants of the same cultivar grown in different situations (see Colour on page 60), it is quite possible that fragrances do too. Grape varieties grown on different soils produce wines of varied bouquet. Frangipanis can be expected to be equally variable in fragrance. Just one example suffices to demonstrate this. The cultivar 'Cyndi Moragne' is described on the Cultivar Register as having a 'faint fragrance', yet a commercial grower in Australia hails it as the most fragrant variety in an extensive collection—perhaps it's a case of mistaken identity.

Richard and Mary Eggenberger, in their *Handbook on Plumeria Culture*, state that the frangipanis and oleanders they grew in India had a better fragrance than the same varieties they had studied elsewhere. To what this could be attributed, they were uncertain. It is perhaps relevant that the best frangipani oil is credited with being produced in India, the country where also some of the world's finest tea is grown. The particular mix of environmental factors, especially soils, altitude and climate, seems to play a significant role.

And just when are fragrances at their best? White-flowered plants can be expected to be most fragrant at night, when their pollinators are at large, but what of coloured flowers? It seems a gross generalisation to say early morning and late afternoons are best. We have noticed, on many occasions, plants to be almost devoid of perfume early in the morning but extremely heady in the heat of the day. Other enthusiasts argue that strong heat is fatal to fragrance because it is rapidly vaporised. Elusive in so many ways, it may truly be said that fragrance lies in the nose of the inhaler. It offers a wealth of opportunities for investigation.

During the course of our other observations in tropical Australia, we have noticed that most *Plumeria obtusa* are fragrant at all times of the day, but occasional trees can be less fragrant in the middle of the day. We have also noticed that, in *Plumeria rubra*, the red varieties are perhaps the least fragrant of all colours, but on picking their fragrance intensifies. That said, of all the varieties we assessed in Australia, it was an unnamed yellow-throated vermilion that was at all times the most fragrant. Varieties with yellow throats have reliably good fragrance, as do apricots/oranges. Many tricolors tend to have poor fragrance in the middle of the day. In other parts of the world, observations may be quite different. One Hawaiian enthusiast maintains that a red, unnamed at the time, is the most fragrant of all varieties. Another researcher, in the flowers' native habitat of the Caribbean, reports that fragrance might be poor in newly opened flowers, but then increases and peaks on the second night.

BELOW: An alluring fragrance, close up confirms equally enchanting flowers.

Perfume and Memory

The sense of smell is intricately linked to memory and emotions because it is processed in the same part of the brain. Aromas trigger associations: suggesting, arousing, disturbing, exciting, etc, and our reactions can be quite personal. In many animals, natural odours called pheromones have been shown to induce behavioural changes.

When commercially available perfumes are applied to the skin, they combine with body odours secreted by skin glands. These are the result of skin bacteria acting on the by-products of our food metabolism. This explains why a particular perfume can smell quite different on different people, and it is a process of trial and error to find which perfumes suit your body and evoke your sense of self-identity—perhaps even induce behavioural changes in those around you.

Up until the 1920s, single flower essences were most common in commercial perfumes. Blends were just becoming possible, for extraction methods and 'fixing' of fragrances were being developed. Fixatives hold the ingredients together and give a perfume its staying power. Fixatives are known as the 'base note' of a perfume, and as a perfume fades they can be detected as the 'last' or 'end note.' When a perfume is first opened, the ingredient of greatest volatility will produce the 'top note'—the first scent you detect. The perfume then moves into the main fragrance theme.

It has been said that a perfumer, using natural talents and highly honed skills, blends selected ingredients much as a composer combines the instruments of an orchestra. Most perfumes today are complex blends of ingredients. The legendary 'Chanel No. 5', created for the House of Chanel, reputedly contains 250 ingredients. Other perfumes may contain many more. The vast majority use Poet's Jasmine (*Jasminum officinale* 'Grandiflorum') or its synthetic equivalent as the foundation. The appeal of synthetic substitutes becomes obvious when you learn that it requires approximately 6 kilograms (13 pounds) of Jasmine flowers to yield just 1 gram (0.03 ounce) of essential oil.

A survey of available perfumes worldwide reveals that few contain frangipani, those that do usually contain *Plumeria alba*. One reference records 'frangipani' perfume as containing sage (*Salvia officinalis*), sandalwood (*Santalum album*), neroli (*Citrus aurantium*) and orris root (*Iris pallida* and *Iris florentina*) essential oils, with musk as a fixative. 'Coco' by Chanel contains frangipani, while 'Narcisse' by Chloe contains *Plumeria rubra* as its dominant note.

Colour

When we speak of frangipani colours, we are dealing with the myriad varieties worldwide of *Plumeria rubra*. In seedlings arising from natural pollination—the bulk of frangipanis you encounter—the variety and patterning of colour is staggering. Add to this the cultivars, plants which earn this status after rigorous evaluation of desirable, stable characteristics, relatively speaking, from the wild or the hand of plant hybridisers, and we have a wealth of beauty based on colour alone. From whites to creams and all shades of yellow, through gold, apricot, orange, pinks and reds, frangipanis bring delight with their flamboyance or restraint—there is a flower to suit every taste.

Then there are bicolors and tricolors in endless patterns, sharp and arresting or muted and beguiling. The generic term 'Fruit Salad' has been given to a range of tricolors that are predominantly orange but with streaks and shadings reminiscent of a mixed fruit salad. These tricolors are also characteristically fragrant—fruity with spicy overtones—and of varying colour throughout the year, most actually changing daily. Their petals tend to curl to different degrees, and their leaves are wavy.

To date, as with roses, true blues have been elusive, but lilacs and lavenders are a step in that direction. This is the focus of current breeding in Thailand with cultivars such as 'Jack's Purple' and 'India' becoming available from specialist nurseries.

A wide colour spectrum exists except for lilac, mauve and blue which is the focus of current research.

Categorising frangipanis on the basis of colour can be initially fraught with difficulty. By convention, though, the predominant hue is the basis of their grouping. A closer inspection will reveal that many individual plants exhibit variations in colour, especially tonal, from flower to flower. Where blooms are shaded they are commonly more intensely coloured, but even within an inflorescence there is often variation. Sunlight brings out colours, but when it is extreme and prolonged, may also bleach blooms, especially within the

Ageing blooms from the same tree makes precise identification difficult. 'Grove Farm' taken at Koko Crater Hawai'i.

red part of the spectrum. Flower colours can also vary from day to day, and the colour of blossoms produced early in the season can be markedly different from those produced late. And if this is not enough to confound any plant varietal pedant, you must also allow for the fact that climate and soil, as well as fertiliser applications, influence flower colour.

Cuttings taken from a plant in a particular climatic zone and planted in a different one will often result in a first-year flowering of a surprisingly different colour. Even when planted within the same area, juvenile plants often differ from their parent tree when flowers first appear. After about the third year,

The undersides of petals are often distinctively patterned, assisting in the identification of cultivars.

colours tend to stabilise to that expected. Seedling-grown plants, on the other hand, are quite unpredictable in every respect—colour being no exception.

In providing evidence of flower colour for registration of cultivars, you need to photograph both the flowers and the inflorescence at 'first full bloom', rather than later in the season. (A flat, dark background such as black velvet is suggested.) Both topside and underside, which is often distinctively patterned, must be photographed. Colour should be determined at a distance of 3 metres (10 feet) and should be classed initially as one of the following: white, yellow, orange, pink or red. (Check for yourself how bi-and tri-colored flowers, viewed from afar, appear to be a single, pure colour.) The Royal Horticultural Society Colour Chart (produced at Kew Gardens, England, in 1966) is used as the standard reference for colour. It is recognised worldwide and should be assessed in daylight, in a bright spot, but not in direct sunlight. Numbered colour swatches allow for accuracy in matching to the petals.

For registration of cultivars the capacity of flowers to retain colour (hue) when exposed to sunlight must also be assessed and rated on a scale of one to five. 'One' indicates noticeable fading by the second morning, while 'five'

indicates no noticeable fading before the flower falls from the tree.

Colour assessment is no simple task. In frangipanis colour bands on both sides of the petals are common, as is a distinct 'throat' or 'eye' of another colour. Shading and prominent veining, often in different colours, contribute to pattern in some varieties. Note, however, that when we see two or more colours together anywhere, we experience the phenomenon known as 'simultaneous contrast'. This, in essence, is the wavelength vibration of each colour impinging on that of the adjacent colour. (Of course, nearby coloured surfaces will also reflect light onto the flower.) The overall perceived colour also varies from one individual to the next. In short, no two people experience the same sensations.

To further complicate the assessment, colour varies under different light intensities, as can occur within different climatic zones, and at higher temperatures hues are intensified. These facts may account in part for the observed changes in colour when a plant is taken from one region to another. (This is why, wherever possible, we have indicated the location of photography in the book.)

And could there be yet further complications? The nature (material and texture) of a surface can influence observed colours, independent of the pigments present. Consider the colour changes seen in a butterfly's wings, birds' feathers and seashells in various lights. Why not the waxy textured frangipani petal? The mutability of the flowers' colours, like the elusiveness of fragrances, is simply another part of their charm.

Texture

The frangipani's flower texture (surface quality), is often described as waxy. It relates closely to their 'substance', a quality that influences their keeping potential and therefore suitability for various uses. As with hue (see above), a 1–5 scale is applied to substance when registering for cultivar status. To test this, freshly picked flowers are placed overnight in water and stored indoors at room temperature around 18°C (65°F). 'One' indicates poor keeping quality when the petals are discoloured or wilted the day following picking. A rating of 'five' is given for flowers not discoloured and not wilted after five nights. Such flowers are considered ideal for lei making, hairpieces, table decorations, weddings, bouquets and posies.

In essence, flowers of heavy texture have good 'substance' and, in turn, good keeping quality. Many people consider 'Celadine' (also known as 'Graveyard Yellow' or 'Common Yellow') to set the benchmark for this quality. Contemporary researchers are giving increasing attention to this in their breeding programs due to the desire for blooms with a high keeping quality.

Leaf Shape

Some gardeners are first attracted to the large lush green leaves of frangipani and there is a great variety of shape in the genus. Observant growers will notice that some have differently shaped leaves. Here are a few standouts:

Spathulate: Commonly found in *Plumeria pudica*, which is often described as having 'paddle-shaped' leaves.

Narrow lanceolate: Commonly found in *Plumeria stenophylla*.

Obtuse: Commonly found in *Plumeria obtusa*, with a blunt and rounded leaf tip.

Elliptical: Commonly found in the *Plumeria rubra* var. *acutifolia* hybrids with a pointed tip.

Undulating margins: Commonly found in the Australian 'Fruit Salad' collection with an interesting wavy leaf edge.

Narrow recurved: Commonly found in *Plumeria sericifolia* with a narrow leaf and curved margins.

TOP LEFT: *Plumeria stenophylla*

TOP CENTRE: *Plumeria pudica*

TOP RIGHT: *Plumeria obtusa*, 'Petite Pink'.

BOTTOM LEFT: Distorted leaves occassionally appear.

BOTTOM CENTRE: *Plumeria rubra var. acutifolia*, the colour of the leaf venation is a good indicator of flower colour. Deep pink to red veins in the leaf are associated with deep pink to red flowers.

BOTTOM RIGHT: Variegated new hybrids, bred in Thailand are slowly trickling in, white and butter-coloured variegations are popular.

Growing

4. Care

Perhaps without peer, frangipanis are minimal care plants. The rewards they bring are far greater than the effort required to grow them well. They are the most amenable of garden subjects. Arguably their only essential requirement is a well-drained situation. A case of 'wet feet' is fatal, and if you can't provide drainage naturally, then it is preferable to either grow them in containers, in which you can create your own growing medium, or to build up your garden soil into raised beds. Where a soil is exceptionally well drained and seems incapable of holding any moisture—such as is found in some situations of pure sand, volcanic ash or disintegrating granitic rock, say in a rock crevice—this may be a perfect place for frangipanis. They are tolerant of the driest of soils—a quality that may ensure their survival in certain areas if global warming continues to bring drought.

Yet conversely, as tropical plants, they are happy with a deluge. Within a garden, they appreciate regular watering and reward it with prolific growth. However, if watering is excessive, studies have shown that vegetative growth will be at the expense of flower production, and prolific soft foliage can invite predation by a whole range of herbivorous creatures.

As with all plant selection, every garden situation must be judged as a unique site, with various conditions within it. If you can't find a suitable spot for a particular species within this, only then should you consider site modification. This results in happier plants and less frustration for the gardener. That said and acknowledged, enthusiasts will go to no end of trouble to create the conditions needed for success. Plumeria passion knows no bounds—and gardeners in frosty climates will go to no end of trouble for their favourites (see Overwintering on page 80).

By the sea, where salt-laden air and strong winds are a limitation to the culture of many species, frangipanis can succeed beyond all expectations.

Naturally, if you can provide shelter from the strongest salty blasts, culture will be easier and the plants less likely to suffer damage in the form of torn and burnt leaves, defoliation and limb breakage. As trees mature, their sturdiness improves and limbs will not break as easily. A warm, wind-sheltered position, in maximum sunshine, is best for flowering. Frangipanis need sun for at least half the day, particularly in the autumn, to ripen the wood and initiate flower buds.

While the trees will tolerate a certain amount of overshadowing, if this is constant and heavy, growth will tend to be spindly and flowers few. The plant will also be more prone to disease and insect attack. Sunshine means health for these sunniest of flowers.

But frangipanis need not be grown in isolation. Providing their canopy is not heavily shaded, they happily accept even dense plantings around them indeed, many gardeners have created delightful compositions for year-round interest. Frangipanis can also be used as support for climbers, which do their own thing while the frangipani may be dormant. The Vanilla Bean Orchid

ABOVE: Frangipanis thrive on neglect. This tree has survived solo for years in this empty paddock. PREVIOUS PAGE: P. 'Kirra Dawn.'

(*Vanilla planifolia*), which is native to the Caribbean region, was traditionally grown against trees such as frangipanis for its support. This climbing orchid produces the pod from which true vanilla is extracted for flavouring in foodstuffs like ice cream and chocolate. In India plantations of *Plumeria alba* are used as a support (see Tropical Climate Companions on page 161).

Feeding

As with all species, naturally dense plantings are more demanding of soil nutrients than are isolated specimens. So supplementary fertilising would be beneficial in these circumstances. Apply fertiliser when the plant is most receptive—immediately prior to the onset of spring growth, with a follow-up application in mid-summer to push the plant along and promote continuation of flowering. Some enthusiasts favour regularly timed, small fertiliser doses throughout the growing season.

Rather than a fertiliser rich in nitrogen, which promotes vegetative growth (foliage), you can opt for one that promotes flowering. Look for a fertiliser high in phosphorus and potassium, and containing trace elements, especially magnesium and iron. The latter helps to keep foliage a healthy green and free of yellowing. Occasional applications of Epsom salts (magnesium sulfate) will be a tonic. Jim Little, a renowned plumeria breeder in Hawai'i, advises that while phosphorus is needed to encourage flowering in well-established plants, fertilisers high in nitrogen are more important for young plants. Composts including manures and organic supplements, such as bone meal and natural minerals like rock phosphate, are excellent soil additives for long-term soil enrichment. Feeding your soil like this cares for the micro-organisms that improve soil structure (aeration and friability). Regular mulching of soils within the drip line of plants, using any available organic material, will also help to retain soil moisture and keep root systems cool on the hottest of days.

If you are using chemical (inorganic) fertilisers, it is always desirable to water the area thoroughly prior to the fertiliser application. This prevents 'burning' of fine feeder roots. Chemical fertilisers unfortunately do nothing to assist soil structure, and, in fact, by making conditions unfavourable for earthworms and other organisms, these chemicals may even work against your otherwise good cultural care.

If growing your frangipanis in containers, a fertiliser program is essential for a good and continuous floral display (see Pots and Planters on page 74). Regular fertiliser application leads to prolific flowering, which will, in turn, encourage a good branch structure, because new growth arises from the base of a spent inflorescence. These laterals are usually well spaced, so the tree naturally establishes a pleasing and balanced branch structure, without the need for any pruning.

Should your plant suffer mechanical damage, in a storm for example, its capacity to re-establish a symmetrically branched form, over time, is truly one of the marvels of nature. There is no need for any interference, other than to remove ragged branch stubs or split branches with a sharp, clean cut, at a 45-degree downward angle—this enables the cut to shed moisture that might encourage fungal attack. Where extensive pruning is undertaken some growers recommend the use of wound sealants.

Transplanting Advanced Plants

With people's desire these days for instant gratification in so many things, including gardens, the frangipani has an undisputed role. Its tolerance of being uprooted, maltreated and relocated in various states of damage, and ability to then survive to flower is truly remarkable. That it can then re-establish itself, filling out growth to create a naturally balanced and umbraceous dome, is even more remarkable. So with just a modicum of effort and care, you can transplant a large, established tree with excellent chances of success. The end of the dormant period, or early spring, is the best season to do this, but it is also possible at other times.

As with transplanting any species, it's best to take as large a root ball as possible, so that the fine feeder roots remain intact. If you have access to machinery to perform this task, the operation is a simple one, once you have severed the roots around the circumference chosen. If you don't have access to the appropriate machinery, the limiting factor will be the weight of root ball that can be manoeuvred with the labour force at hand. In these cases it pays to not be too ambitious. Even a root ball of 0.75 metres (2.5 feet) is very heavy when the tree itself is added. But the reality of most hand removals, especially where the soil is a sandy loam, is that a great deal of soil will fall away, leaving many roots exposed. Keep as many roots intact as possible and cleanly trim those that tear. Transplant the tree to the new location without delay, where, ideally, you have pre-dug the planting hole. Position the tree carefully, and backfill with good loamy material, building it up to the pre-existing ground level. Water the tree in thoroughly, and secure it back to three widely spaced stakes, to ensure that there is no chance of the tree rocking in wind. The tree will re-establish its roots rapidly.

While the tree will need a reasonably moist soil for re-establishment, be careful not to over-water. As previously stated, with frangipanis it is better to under-water than over-water. They have a remarkable inbuilt capacity in their fleshy stems to survive water stress, but they will quickly succumb to root rot in waterlogged conditions. Because of this, if you want to transplant a tree to a site of heavy clay or otherwise poorly drained soil, you will have more chance than of success if, rather planting into a hole, you sit the roots on top of the ground, then fill around them with free-draining material. In effect, you are mounding around the roots, being careful to avoid placing soil above the level at which the tree previously grew. Again, secure the trunk and water well.

Of course, it is not always possible to transplant a tree immediately, in which case pot up the tree in a suitable capacity tub for re-establishment. Guying back to stakes will still usually be necessary. If there is to be a delay of only a few weeks before the tree can be planted, it is possible to 'heel it in' in the meantime, simply by resting it on the ground and piling moist sawdust, timber shavings or other loose absorbent material over the roots to prevent them drying out.

Frangipani branches can be brittle, so take special care with them. It may be desirable to cut out some branches to render the tree more manageable. These removals can assist markedly in the tree's handling and re-establishment, and the tree can replace its branches surprisingly quickly.

Under hot conditions, reduce moisture loss by spraying the tree with an anti-transpirant. Many commercial products are available. So don't be daunted by the prospect transplanting even quite large trees. The chances of success are high, and you will have the satisfaction of retrieving trees that perhaps would otherwise be destroyed.

In author John Stowar's garden, heavily pruned and recently transplanted, the inclination of this 66-year-old tree will accentuate both its age and gnarled form.

How to Transplant, Balinese-style

In Bali frangipanis grow brilliantly pretty much anywhere. They are often transported as mature trees, with a root ball no bigger than a bucket. Wedged into place and staked securely, they are left to their own devices, a technique we have mimicked many times at home with great success. As a visitor to Bali, you can often see huge frangipani trees piled high on rickety trucks on their way to new gardens; no leaves, no roots and seemingly no possibility of surviving other than from a will to live. But after a few months in the ground, they magically start producing new leaves and often flower the same year. Their reputation as the 'Tree of Life' is well deserved.

LEFT: Recently transplanted frangipanis in Bali are stabilised using bamboo supports.
BELOW: Transplanting mature trees is surprisingly successful. Ensure as much as possible of the root system is intact. Secure the trunk to the crane with a hessian sling. Voila—an instant focal point for your garden.

Pots and Planters

Through choice or by necessity, more and more gardeners are enjoying the pleasures of container gardening. And frangipanis make exceptional container subjects. In climates of borderline suitability, decks, balconies and paved courtyards or patios provide a warm microclimate, which facilitates frangipani culture. If there is any disadvantage to container gardening it is the fact that plants in containers dry out more rapidly than do plants in the ground. This generally restricts one's opportunities to go away, unless watering can be left to friends or a reliable irrigation system is installed. However, as frangipanis are able to draw upon moisture stored in their fleshy stems, they can survive prolonged periods of neglect, even during the height of summer. In hot, westerly aspects, where few plants tolerate the conditions, frangipanis will thrive. In large containers and with good culture, they can reach tree dimensions, providing years of beauty, perfume and a welcome canopy against summer heat.

Commercial growers are increasing their efforts to select and develop compact varieties that will be well suited to container gardening. These plants, along with those that naturally develop a strongly branching habit, make ideal subjects.

Frangipanis often flower prolifically when pot bound.

Container Selection

If you intend growing plants to tree size, then select the largest containers you can accommodate, preferably those wider than they are deep. Those of simple shape, with straight or splayed sides are best. This facilitates plant extraction, which may be required for potting on, transplanting into the open ground or simply root-trimming.

Plastic pots retain moisture much more effectively than terracotta or concrete, and they are also better if 'potting on' is necessary, because the roots do not attach themselves to the plastic pots. If you don't like the look of plastic, sit them within another container more to your liking (see also Balconies and Terraces on page 148).

Drainage

To ensure free drainage, use a good quality commercial potting mix or prepare your own. Three parts sand to one part organic material, such as peatmoss, cocopeat or compost, is ideal. Where weight is a consideration, a lighter suitable medium is two parts perlite to one part peat or similar organic material. Check that the container drainage holes are adequate. Inadequately drained containers commonly cause waterlogged conditions. This is fatal for frangipanis. It is also best to avoid placing saucers or trays under the containers. If drip trays are essential, stand the container on a layer of pebbles and make sure all water has evaporated from the tray before the plant is watered again. Outdoors it is a good practice to stand the container on three or four pavers or bricks, to elevate it and thereby reduce the likelihood of drainage holes becoming blocked. Alternatively you could elect to construct raised planters, which are often a good option in small gardens.

After repotting it is essential to keep the plant stable with three bamboo stakes.

Feeding Potted Plants

Some enthusiasts maintain that a frangipani must become almost pot-bound before it flowers prolifically. Certainly, it is well recorded in horticultural research that plants under stress are likely to flower well, as a last-ditch attempt to set seed and so perpetuate the species. However, if a plant's root system fills its container and the plant is not fed, it will eventually languish. All its nutrients are contained within the pot. Those nutrients that the plant doesn't use leach out with watering, so must be replenished over time. Several options are available and the method adopted will depend on your capacities and commitment:

Regularly feed the plant by applying soluble fertiliser to both the foliage and the potting medium. Alternatively, incorporate fertiliser regularly in the top of the pot when you top dress.

Every couple of years scrape and remove the top 75 millimetres (3 inches) of potting mix, and replace it with fresh mix into which fertiliser is incorporated. This is best undertaken in early spring. Mulch continuously with rich organic material.

Every couple of years, ideally late in the dormant period, remove the plant from the pot. Trim the root ball by 50 millimetres (2 inches) or so and repot into fresh enriched mix.

Over time it will be necessary to pot on all plants except those in very large containers; all potted plants must be fed. A good technique, if somewhat laborious, is to soak the plant thoroughly and divide the root ball into six wedges, like segments of a pie when viewed from above. Using a combination of scraping away potting mix and root pruning (with a pruning saw or large knife), remove two opposite wedges for the full depth of the root ball. Replace these segments with fresh, enriched potting mix. The following year, remove two further opposite segments, and in the third year remove the last two opposite segments. From then on, rotate removal of opposite wedges, in sequence, annually. Late spring or early summer is the best time for this.

Containerised plants should always be mulched diligently. The mulch becomes a protective layer between feeding roots and climatic extremes, which are more pronounced for potted plants than those in the ground. Don't forget that these plants are totally dependent on the growing medium, the pot's exposure to light, wind and rainfall, and the culture given by the gardener. A potted plant has limited opportunities to do its own thing, save break through the pot. If the container and the growing medium have been well selected, and the container well positioned, the ongoing plant care will make all the difference between a plant just surviving or flourishing.

All things being equal, a plant in a small container can never match the performance of one with ample pot capacity. A plant that is watered and fertilised only when the gardener feels moved to do this, will never compare with one that has constant vigilance and eternal commitment from the gardener. And every plant is an individual. Its own personality should be assessed. Some cultivars are naturally robust; others are relative weaklings in spite of possessing the capacity to produce beguiling blooms (see Cultivars on page 108).

The size of the plant will largely determine its requirements for water and fertiliser. Moisture meters can be helpful. When exposed to drying winds, a containerised plant will need more frequent watering than one that is sheltered but otherwise comparable in every respect. Evening watering is most effective—and environmentally sound—because evaporation is less. For the same reason, foliar fertilising is best carried out at the end of the day. This application method also overcomes the problem of fertiliser leaching away when a potted plant is watered frequently.

Pruning

When frangipanis grow well, and perhaps exceed all expectations with their vigour, it is not uncommon to hear the complaint that a tree has become too tall, with its floral display visible only to birds flying overhead. This is easily corrected by lopping—even to a stump. It is not possible to be too severe with pruning. Because wounds on frangipanis rapidly heal over, pruning can be safely undertaken at any time. It is perhaps easier when a plant is dormant,

Well-pruned trees at Pearl City Community Garden, Hawai'i.

if for no other reason than that it is easier to access the branches, which are also lighter, and that there is little to no bleeding of sap. However, if you want the tree to refurbish quickly, a late spring/early summer prune is best.

Cut always at just above a prominent leaf scar, to minimise the likelihood of any dieback (see Troubleshooting on page 80). A 45-degree cut is best (see Propagation on page 94).

Depending on the shape and branching of the tree, it may be possible to reduce only part of its height, leaving the rest for pruning the following year.

Frangipanis respond reliably after heavy lopping, even when it's back to a stump.

This will ensure that at least some flowers can be enjoyed in the current year. Outside the tropics it is common for a heavily pruned tree to have no flowers that year. However, the following year it should return to its normal flowering habit.

Inflorescences form at the branch tips and immediately below. Anything from one to six, or so, new shoots develop, depending on variety. Each shoot potentially produces an inflorescence the following year, but if conditions are not favourable, this may be delayed till the following year.

Cutting back hard, almost to ground level, can even rejuvenate aged and spindly specimens. If such drastic action is not your style, and you simply would like an additional branch or two in specific locations, use fine sandpaper to rub the branch gently, immediately above the closest leaf scar—the crescent-shape mark on a branch left when a leaf has fallen. This may stimulate a new branch to grow (see also Pools on page 145).

OPPOSITE TOP: Crown-lifted trees will lift their canopies to maximise the space beneath their branches.

OPPOSITE BELOW LEFT: Poorly crown-lifted trees will make new shoots from pruned stumps. Avoid this by pruning closer to the main trunk.

OPPOSITE BELOW RIGHT: Pruning wounds gradually heal over time. Well-pruned 'crown-lifted' trees are an asset in a garden setting.

5. Troubleshooting

It is well known that frangipanis are relatively fuss free, but in some cases and under some extreme climates they will need additional care. The process of 'overwintering' the technique of moving frangipanis into protected environments over winter, will only be required for those living in very cold climates. General pest and disease information is necessary and will change depending on your microclimate, location and culture.

Overwintering in Cold Climates

A garden affords the purest of human pleasures.
It is the greatest refreshment to the spirits of man without
which buildings and palaces are but gross handiworks.

Francis Bacon

Gardeners from warmer climes might marvel at the procedures gardeners of frostier areas undertake to protect their frangipanis from winter. Why not grow something more suitable? Unthinkable! Such is people's love for these plants, that the measures they take to protect the trees from frost know no bounds. It is a small price to pay for the pleasure they bring.

Prior to the anticipated first frost of autumn, the besotted enthusiast will simply lift the plants, holus-bolus, from the garden. Often they will use a machine for the task. No need to stress too much about damaging some roots

Unknown cultivar,
Sydney, Australia.

Overwintering shelter, Tweed Heads, Australia.

or leaving others behind in the process: frangipanis have notoriously small root runs and are tough. More committed enthusiasts will hand dig and lift plants to avoid the risk of damage. The measures appropriate depend on the particular situation. If soil adheres, especially around the fine feeding roots, so much the better—although some growers maintain soil retention is unnecessary.

Transfer the plant to a warm garage, basement or spare room where temperatures do not drop below about 0°C (32°F). If the floor is concrete, first put down a cover of cardboard or similar insulation. In some areas all you will need is a veranda, covered patio or even a decent eave. A cool greenhouse is not advised, as in cold areas it will retain moisture and the dampness will increase the likelihood of black tip fungus (see page 90). Defoliated plants take up little room, so can be stacked two or three high.

Did You Know?

Peter Valder, in his book *The Garden Plants of China*, reveals that at the Pavilion of Admirable Fragrance, Gongwangfu Tea House, in Beijing—an eighteenth-century mansion, with what many consider to be northern China's finest city garden—special 'flower caves' were used for protecting frost-tender plants such as frangipanis.

Covering the plants with an old rug is also helpful, but do not use material, such as plastic sheeting, that does not breathe. Lightweight and breathable blankets of spun polyester, known as 'horticultural fleece' are also available. Some gardeners wrap the stems in hessian or cloth, or cover them with granulated foam or similar insulating material. Where temperatures approach freezing, dedicated gardeners will also cover the plants with loose, coarse mulch such as straw. Leave the plants alone until spring, then, when you are reasonably confident that frosts have finished, replant and water in well. It's as simple as that, although temporary frost protection is advisable both during establishment and whenever frost threatens. Remember that winter is the natural dormant season for most frangipanis, so expect most if not all foliage to yellow and fall. Do not be tempted to give any water during this overwintering.

Because the initiation of dormancy is related to shortening day length, some enthusiasts place their plants in artificially lit situations to encourage flowering through autumn, even when the plants have been lifted from the ground. Others continue lighting through the winter months with fluorescent or 'grow lights', convinced that this helps to initiate flower buds for spring.

For the frangipani enthusiast who doesn't wish to follow the above path, a more traditional approach to overwintering might be adopted. It is that employed in England and Europe since the Renaissance. Potted citrus were transferred to 'orangeries'—light-filled, heated rooms. The amount of essential light they received was directly proportional to the amount of glass the household could afford in the structure. As glass became less expensive, this room developed into the 'conservatory'.

Nowadays, with the availability of large sheets of plate glass, many houses and apartments have rooms with sufficient light and central heating for plants. Frangipanis can flower happily indoors, but accept that they are not indoor plants in the same sense as ferns and palms; they still require good air circulation, sunshine and occasional drenching rain to remain healthy and vigorous. Return them outdoors on a regular basis, unless you can provide full-on glasshouse conditions. To facilitate the movement of heavy potted plants, you can sit each pot on a base with castors and place it somewhere that does not have steps to reach it.

With all species that are overwintered, whether containerised or not, the same rules apply. In the weeks prior to overwintering, reduce watering and cease all feeding. You do not want any soft growth, which is especially vulnerable to damage. Once the plants are reinstated following the overwintering, apply water and fertiliser to encourage vigorous new growth. In windy situations it may also be necessary to stake your plants securely until they are re-established or better still, provide wind barriers.

Pests and Diseases

It would be wonderful to be able to state with confidence that frangipanis are foolproof, that nothing bothers them, that with even haphazard care they will thrive. But every living plant is mortal, and some 'gardeners' can be blind to the most obvious of cultural requirements. With this in mind, frangipanis really are minimal-care plants assuming their basic needs are met, namely a sunny, frost-free situation with excellent drainage. If they are also provided with occasional fertiliser, regular mulching and supplementary water when drought conditions prevail, even those with marginal interest in the natural world won't be able to resist their charms.

With globalisation of the agricultural and horticultural trades—as well as increased international travel—the reality now is that pests and diseases hitherto unknown in a region can appear at any time, in spite of all precautions. An area free of a particular pest or disease is lucky to remain that way for long. Healthy and vigorously growing plants have the best resistance to potential problems, while a gardener who keeps a watchful eye for changes in condition can respond quickly to potential problems. This may involve no more than a stroll through the garden every few days to remove any incipient problem, perhaps simply by plucking a few leaves and disposing of them thoughtfully or diligently removing dieback at branch tips. Prompt action can avert the need for more drastic measures down the track. However, never place diseased and infected plant material in the compost bin.

More extensive health issues obviously warrant a greater effort, but in every instance, before rushing for the spray can, consider the cultural needs of the plant. The problem may have been precipitated by something as simple as impeded drainage, deficient air circulation or excessive shading from an overly vigorous nearby tree. Unusual and extreme weather conditions also occur. Those who garden outside the preferred environments of the species, must accept that their frangipanis will have more susceptibility to pests and diseases. And it is a regrettable reality that the garden of an enthusiast who cannot resist adding yet another plant to an already extensive collection, is more at risk to pest infestations and disease eruptions than one that includes only a few specimens—more so when the plants are crowded.

Diseases can spread in unexpected ways. We have observed honeybees collecting the golden spores of frangipani rust from heavily infested foliage, filling their pollen sacks and dispersing the disease far and wide as they foraged. When spraying fungicide to address this problem, it is essential to spray all the foliage on both sides, as well as to drench the soil after having removed fallen leaves. Some success has been achieved with a twice-weekly spray application of one teaspoon of baking soda dissolved in 1 litre (2 pints) water. Do a thorough winter clean up of fallen leaves that may harbour the rust spores. During summer, avoid wetting foliage in the late afternoon.

Even hot sun, which frangipanis normally relish, can be the cause of sun-scorch on foliage and sunburn on stems, especially when a plant is relocated from nursery conditions or a place of semi-shade to full sun. Watering the plant by overhead spray in the heat of the day exacerbates this. Of course sun-scorch may be nothing more than disfigurement, and the plant may continue to flower and grow well in spite of it. This sometimes also occurs near the coast, when the plant has been exposed to salt- and wind-burn.

Rotting stems and roots, commonly the result of poor drainage or overwatering, should be cut back to healthy wood, well clear of any sign of the dieback, at the first opportunity. In stems this may also be due to low temperatures. A precautionary fungicidal dusting of every wound is recommended.

A pesticide-free garden will encourage allies such as frogs to take up residence.

Pest-repellent Planting

Using toxic sprays to kill pests has a major flaw. It often kills the 'goodies' as well as the 'baddies'. The 'goodies' include natural predators of the same pests you are trying to control. A better method is to grow plants that deter pests from attacking—usually by emitting strong scents—to mask the plant being infested. Others repel pests from the area, while some can be ingredients in environmentally friendly sprays. Fragrant, ground-covering herbs may suit the task. They are included in the following summary.

Pests and Diseases Summary

Pests and diseases are not as common on frangipani as other tropical plants, however from time to time, problems occur. Here are the pests and diseases known to affect frangipanis, the symptoms and possible cures. In no time your frangipani will look refreshed.

Aphids/Greenfly

DESCRIPTION	Sucking insects that suck sap out of plant.
SYMPTOM	Congregations of tiny sap-sucking insects especially on new growth, which can shrivel and distort new leaves. They produce 'honeydew', a sugary exudate, which promotes sooty mould fungus and attracts ants.
TREATMENT	• Dislodge with water jet.
	• Encourage small birds and predatory ladybirds.
	• Include fragrant herbs in garden, such as garlic, onions, lavender, peppermint, spearmint, rosemary, fennel and nasturtium.

Whitefly

DESCRIPTION Sucking insects that suck sap out of plant.

SYMPTOM Congregations of tiny white flies on the underside of leaves. Honeydew exudate promotes sooty mould fungus and attracts ants.

TREATMENT
- Dislodge with water jet.
- Spray with organic insecticidal soap.
- Include fragrant herbs in the garden such as basil, lavender and rosemary.
- Use a sticky trap to attract whitefly away from tree.

Scale

DESCRIPTION White spots on stem. Small, waxy, shell-like insect that sucks plant sap.

SYMPTOM Small round or oval wax spots on stem tips and leaves. Honeydew exudate promotes sooty mould fungus.

TREATMENT
- Encourage predatory ladybirds.
- Spray with horticultural grade spraying oil early in the day.

Thrips

DESCRIPTION Small insect with scraping mouthparts.

SYMPTOM Flower buds may not open and may fall off. Bleeding of sap from tip overnight.

TREATMENT
- Allow spider webs and spiders, their natural predators, to be part of the garden. The thrips may be pollinating.

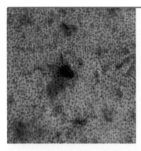

Spidermite

DESCRIPTION   Sucking insects that suck sap out of plant. Impossible to see with naked eye.

SYMPTOM   Mottled and curled leaves. Small webs may be visible on growth tips.

TREATMENT
- Dislodge affected area with water jet, especially under leaves.
- Release predatory mites.
- Spray with insecticidal soap or miticide.

Longicorn, or Long Horn Borer, Beetle/Stem Borer

DESCRIPTION   The grub of the longhorn beetle travels inside the stem and eats the stem from the inside.

SYMPTOM   Small pinholes in stems with sawdust-like material or a dark exudate caused by larvae burrowing under the bark especially in stressed plants. Seen as wilted limbs and foliage.

TREATMENT
- Cut out affected area and destroy it.
- Fertilise and water plant to improve vigour.

Macadamia Leafminer

DESCRIPTION   Semi-transparent tunnels appear through the leaf.

SYMPTOM   Larvae of a small moth burrow within the leaf, causing a blistering of the surface that ultimately looks scorched as if by fire. Problem is worse near rainforest and in wind-sheltered areas.

TREATMENT
- Remove affected leaves as soon as damage is noticed.

Fruitspotting Bug

DESCRIPTION Small orange bug with distinctive spots on the tail.

SYMPTOM Both nymphs and adults of this native Australian bug suck sap, causing sunken dark spots and brown disfiguration. Trees near bushland are especially vulnerable in northern Australia.

TREATMENT • Drench with soap solution.

Snails and slugs

DESCRIPTION Gastropods with rasping tongue with or without shell.

SYMPTOM Chewed stems.

TREATMENT • Pick off and destroy pests.

• Spread spent coffee grounds around base of trunk.

• Place traps for collection (halved and hollowed oranges are excellent).

Mealy Bug

DESCRIPTION A tiny insect with a cotton wool covering that sucks plant sap.

SYMPTOM Insects congregate on leaves and stems, and secrete honeydew; if abundant they will weaken plant.

TREATMENT • Cut out or remove entire branch.

• Spray with a low toxic systemic insecticide.

Grasshopper

DESCRIPTION Green or brown insects with large hopping legs, wings and large jaws.

SYMPTOM Chewed leaves

TREATMENT • There is little control as grasshoppers move on very quickly after damage is done. Use a low toxic systemic insecticide as prevention if grasshoppers are prevalent.

Black Tip Fungus/Black Leg/ Black Rot/Stem Rot

DESCRIPTION Fungus is usually seen in spring.

SYMPTOM Growing tip becomes soft and black as the inside rots away and the point will die back either without stopping or until the plant compartmentalises the fungal attack. Cold conditions over winter will exacerbate this problem.

TREATMENT
- Cut out blackened tip to clean wood.
- Drench soil and stems with a fungicide as soon as apparent. Fungicides with the active ingredient bayleton or benomyl are effective.
- Dust cuttings with fungicide before potting or use a root hormone containing fungicide.
- Use perlite for rooting cuttings for fast drainage.
- Do not overwater rooting cuttings.
- Check for the disease by squeezing the bases of your cuttings—they should be firm.
- During winter storage keep your plants as warm as possible, at least above 10°C (50°F).
- Improve air circulation to reduce humidity around plant.
- If all else fails, try taking another cutting from healthy wood.

NOTE: Stem rot occurs while trying to root cuttings or during winter storage. Stem rot moves quickly and is nearly always fatal to cuttings. Cool temperatures and wet soil are the favourite conditions for this fungus. Rooting and newly rooted cuttings during their first winter are at the highest risk. Once the cutting has survived a few winters, it is usually not a problem. Mature trees can also lose branches from stem rot or freeze damage. They look almost the same and the only treatment is pruning off the affected areas. After the stem has died back, new growth buds will become active below the dieback point and will replace this growing point (as seen above).

Dieback

DESCRIPTION Stems dieback in canopy.

SYMPTOM Stems become dark, papery and hollow, more likely to be noticed in winter after leaf fall.

TREATMENT
- Cut out all affected branches, back to clean, healthy wood.
- Increase air circulation around branches by thinning.

Rootrot

DESCRIPTION Root fungus in soil.

SYMPTOM Wilted foliage or stems.

TREATMENT
- Spray with Phosacid over leaves.
- Upend potted plant and trim diseased roots and replant into better-drained soil.
- Improve drainage or move the plant into a drier garden position.

Powdery Mildew

DESCRIPTION Fungus on leaf.

SYMPTOM A white mould or light discoloured patches start to appear and spread on leaves.

TREATMENT
- Apply a general fungicide to the foliage.
- Improve air circulation by thinning out canopy.

Sooty Mould

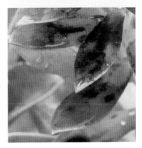

DESCRIPTION Fungus on leaf.

SYMPTOM Black sooty patches develop on leaves that usually follow sucking insects such as aphids, whitefly or thrip, growing on the sugars they secrete.

TREATMENT
- Treat insect pests and spray with horticultural grade spraying oil early in the day.

Rust

DESCRIPTION   Fungus (*Coleosporium dominguense*)

SYMPTOM   Warm and humid conditions encourage orange 'pollen-like' fungus spores in pustules on the underside of leaves in late summer/early autumn. Upper leaf remains brown and discoloured. Premature leaf drop may occur.

TREATMENT
- Clean up and dispose of all fallen leaves.
- Increase air circulation by thinning out branches.
- Drench foliage (both sides) and soil with fungicide.
- General fungicides will slow disease. Spray after leaf fall avoiding reinfection for the next year.
- Avoid watering foliage in late afternoon, and water the ground not the foliage.
- In smaller gardens remove infected lower leaves and dispose of them thoughtfully in the bin and not compost, as they will reinfect the soil. Spray the foliage with soapy/detergent water; after several hours, wash off with water jet.
- Recent studies show fungicides with the active ingredient oxycarboxin, bayleton or benomyl are more effective than other fungicides.

NOTE: Rust is becoming more prevalent in Florida, USA, and Queensland and New South Wales, Australia and is likely to spread further through the subtropical and warm temperate zones. It does not kill a frangipani but can lead to the rapid defoliation of a tree. Rust spores are spread by rain.

Aerial or Adventitious Roots

DESCRIPTION Small roots above soil level.

SYMPTOM Branch splits to reveal 1mm wide white roots. Can be at trunk level above soil or higher up.

TREATMENT
- No treatment. However if this happens to new cuttings and below the aerial roots the stem starts to wither, cut off just below the aerial roots and make a new cutting. The aerial roots will become the new root system.

Sunburnt Leaves

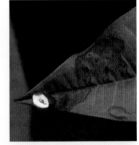

DESCRIPTION Sap burns within leaf leaving scorch marks on leaf.

SYMPTOM Brown burnt patches appear on topside on leaf.

TREATMENT
- Remove affected leaves when threat of hot weather subsides; they should remain until then to protect the plant from further hot days.

Green Looper Caterpillar

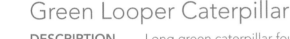

DESCRIPTION Long green caterpillar found under leaves.

SYMPTOM Eaten leaves.

TREATMENT
- Spray with an organic biological control for caterpillars.

Yellowing Leaves

DESCRIPTION Nutrient deficiency due to depleted or alkaline soil (alkaline soil locks up nutrients).

SYMPTOM Leaves start to yellow and the veins remain green.

TREATMENT
- Build up the organic matter such as composted animal manures in the soil.
- Test the pH of the soil and treat accordingly. Frangipanis prefer neutral to slightly acidic soil pH.

6. Propagation

One frangipani is never enough, so it is just as well they are one of the easiest flowers in the plant kingdom to replicate. The easiest reliable method to obtain specific varieties is by cuttings. Seedlings are variable and occasionally will produce exciting developments but never the same genetics as the parent tree from which the seed was collected.

Cuttings

Propagating a frangipani by taking a cutting is simplicity itself. Few plants are as amenable to propagation from cuttings as are frangipanis. Experienced gardeners take cuttings year-round, but if you are unsure of your skills, the ideal time is at the end of the dormant period, at the onset of the natural growth cycle in spring.

Select a plump, healthy-looking branch end. Cuttings of thick stems from vigorous plants will flower earlier than those from less vigorous plants. They also produce larger flowers. The terminal growing bud should ideally look shiny and 'moist', and, although you can take cuttings from branches with green bark, mature grey bark is desirable. Cleanly saw off a piece, up to about 300 millimetres (12 inches) long. If this can be taken just below a leaf scar or branch junction, so much the better, as this encourages the plant to be sturdy. A cut at 45 degrees is ideal for two reasons: it allows rain and dew to drain away from the wound on the mother tree, discouraging any dieback in the branch; and the cutting itself will have a large area of exposed stem. The cambium (the tissue just below the bark) is what actively produces roots, and an oblique cut exposes maximum cambium.

Place this cutting in a dry and shaded spot for 10 to 14 days, during which time the wound will dry out and heal over. 'Callus' tissue may also become apparent. This is a white-cream warty outgrowth from the cut, from which roots will emerge once the cutting is planted.

Prior to planting, some growers routinely dip the cutting in a rooting compound mixed with a fungicide. Other growers find no need for this, and some enthusiasts maintain that the procedure actually impedes the rooting process. It is advisable that every gardener experiment to find what is most successful under the prevailing conditions where he or she lives.

Polystyrene boxes are excellent containers to strike a large number of cuttings.

Soil for Propagating

It is essential that the soil into which the cutting is placed be as free draining as possible. Garden soil with high clay content is generally too heavy, and, in fact, most soils are inadequately drained for propagating frangi cuttings. Perlite, especially that of a coarse texture is ideal, but it is best to use a mix of three parts perlite to one part of organic material, such as peatmoss, compost etc. Fill a container, a pot, around 300 millimetres (12 inches) in diameter is ideal, then thoroughly soak the soil to facilitate settlement. Once it is drained, insert the cutting to a depth of 75 millimetres (3 inches) or thereabouts. Firm the propagating soil around the cutting, then place the container in a warm to hot, wind-sheltered spot, preferably covered to protect it from deluges. Here it must be left undisturbed until rooting has taken place. In cooler climates stone mulch can help to establish a warm microclimate.

Watering Cuttings

The newly planted cutting must not be watered again until the soil is quite dry. Only then should it be watered, and sparingly at that. As a rule of thumb, in the absence of rain, one cup of water per week should be sufficient until the cutting is leafing out and clearly growing. In reality it depends on the nature of the soil used and the evaporation rate experienced at the time.

A Word of Warning

More cuttings, and plants, are lost because of overwatering than from any other cause. Proper care of a frangipani cutting verges almost on 'neglect', and accounts for the phenomenon in horticulture known affectionately as 'Mug's Luck'. Dispense with any feelings of concern for a moisture-starved cutting. Incipient wrinkling of the bark is a clear indication that more moisture is needed, but this rarely occurs. Far more common is a cutting that looks normal, but in fact is a hollow shell—the centre having been destroyed by fungus encouraged through overwatering. Should this occur, all is not necessarily lost. It may be possible to save the cutting by reducing it back severely, clear of any sign of the dieback and starting the whole process again by first drying out the wound.

Accept too that the ease with which cuttings strike varies considerably amongst varieties or cultivars. A few are quite recalcitrant. In these cases rooting hormone powders will improve the strike rate, and some growers use these as a matter of course.

Avoid any temptation to lift out cuttings to check development of the root system. It is not uncommon for a cutting to be apparently actively growing— even flowering—long before any roots have formed. Disturbing the cutting will set back its establishment and may even kill it. Patience will be rewarded with a sturdy and vigorous plant. Should flowers appear, simply enjoy them and look forward to the foliage following. Some nursery people remove any flowers so that the plant puts all energy into foliage and root development, but because a frangipani loses so much sap from any wound, it is questionable which practice has less impact.

Girdling and Air-layering

To improve the strike rate of varieties that are difficult to strike, 'girdling' can be beneficial. This involves removing a strip of bark approximately 10 millimetres (0.3 inches) wide, down to the cambium around the entire stem circumference. This is done about one month prior to removing the cutting, which should be taken just below the girdle. Girdle only mature grey wood. Then treat it as you would any cutting (see above).

An extension of girdling, especially useful for hard-to-strike varieties, is the technique known as air-layering. In this method, best done in spring, the girdled branch is surrounded with moist peatmoss, cocopeat or similar, then wrapped in plastic and bound tightly at each side, bonbon-style. After three months or so, a mass of roots should fill this wrapping, which can then be removed and the new 'plant' severed from the tree. Planted carefully, this is arguably the most sure-fire technique for propagating any variety.

Top Tips

Rooting should take place in late spring, early summer. It is most successful at 15.5°C (60°F). Don't plant new cuttings any deeper than 75 millimetres (3 inches), and do not water cuttings while they are rooting. Dark reds and Singapores are the hardest to root. You don't need to use root hormone. Water when you see new leaves from your cutting; this could take some time.

Larger Cuttings

For gardeners of impatient disposition, it is possible to grow a frangipani from a branch of up to, say, 2 metres (6 feet) long. The branch may have many 'arms'. To prepare it for planting, cut the main stem as outlined above, but also wound the sides of that part which will be inserted into the propagating soil. A long cutting will need up to 600 millimetres (2 feet) inserted for stability. Scraping a pruning saw or secateurs vertically along this length around the stem to expose part of the cambium is a simple procedure and may help to stimulate cambial activity. Leave the cutting for two weeks to heal over before planting.

With long cuttings it is imperative that every precaution be taken to prevent the cutting from rocking or moving during establishment. Staking and tying

back is desirable and should be retained for at least a year.

Rather than dig a deep hole for a large cutting, a useful alternative is to create a mound of soil and plant the cutting within this. This is an especially useful technique in poorly drained soils (see Transplanting Advanced Plants on page 71).

Vince Winkel, a designer and former parks curator at the Flecker Botanic Gardens in Cairns, Australia, advised us that, during his many years working in the tropics, he had great success with so-called 'fence post' cuttings. This involves installing a fence post or steel star picket at the position intended for the tree, and tying large cuttings (3–5 metres, 10–16 feet) securely to the stake, with the dried cut end resting on the ground. Spread around this a layer of sand, up to 100 millimetres (4 inches) in depth. Tie securely with webbing tape, or similar, making sure that you insert a layer of material to separate the stake and trunk, to prevent rubbing in strong winds. Remove the tie and the stake after two years. This is essential to avoid damage to the trunk.

Long, leafy cuttings have had their leaves cut rather than pulled. This prevents loss of sap and speeds the healing process.

Cuttings Taken When in Leaf

Some growers have achieved excellent results during the growing season with leafy cuttings. For evergreen plants and those sourced for cuttings when in leafy growth, all leaves are best removed from the cutting prior to planting. Pulling off leaves causes maximum sap loss, but this can be minimised by cutting off each leaf leaving a stub of petiole of approximately 20 millimetres (0.75 inches). Allow the whole cutting to dry out (as outlined above) before planting.

If glasshouse or misting facilities are available, short 'leafy' cuttings of up to say 200 millimetres (8 inches) and treated with rooting hormone, will strike readily. For all cuttings, rooting is promoted with 'bottom heat'. For the small-scale enthusiast, the top of a water heater is ideal.

We also know of a commercial frangipani enthusiast who has had success with cuttings of any length taken in full leaf. The leaves were removed using secateurs, leaving a stub of petiole about 20 millimetres (0.75 inches) long, and the cuttings placed upright in dappled shade for five to eight weeks. By that time the cut ends have swollen and developed callus. The cuttings are then planted and thoroughly watered. For the longer cuttings, careful staking is essential to prevent 'rocking' in the wind during establishment.

A Few Words to the Would-be Frangipani Thief

So strong is the urge to possess the frangipani, that one could easily yield to temptation. And this is in spite of the abundance of plants, rooted and unrooted cuttings, and seeds available through nurseries and collectors. Gardeners are usually generous people and only too happy to share their enthusiasm for a particular plant. So when you spy a plant you fancy, approach the owner. Usually he or she will be only too happy to oblige; perhaps more so with frangipanis than with other plants. There is certainly a growing fraternity amongst those hooked on these fabulous beauties. But be aware too, that you may meet with rebuttal if an outstanding tree is the cause of countless daily requests. There has to be a limit.

That said, unscrupulous developers and unthinking owners have been known to destroy beautiful trees, even large, old specimens. If you find out that a tree is to be destroyed, we suggest that you take every measure to save it. At the very least, you could obtain cuttings from 'at risk' plants of uncommon beauty. Even after a tree has been destroyed or removed, there may still be hope of a cutting. Take a walk in the neighbourhood. There is every chance that the same variety grows in a nearby garden, because you won't have been the first to appreciate its charms.

Propagation by Seed

Because there is so much variety in plants produced from seeds—even in seeds collected from one seed pod—the practice of naming seedlings as identical to the parent tree is wrong. It is an invalid and wholly inaccurate method of obtaining the same cultivar. Nurseries following this practice are unethical. The only way to guarantee a variety is 'true to type' is to propagate by vegetative means, that is: cuttings, grafts or tissue culture.

That said, it is from seedlings that new varieties arise, so your endeavours could be rewarded with a variety so outstanding that it warrants registration as a new cultivar. In our minds, this contributes to making the world a more beautiful place. You may even 'get the bug' and explore the rather skilled processes of collecting and transferring pollen to create a fully planned cross from known parents. To date, the numbers of cultivars in existence of this type are very few.

The following steps will help ensure success:

Step 1

Observe the pods you have selected daily as they mature over nine months or so. Once ripe they split open to release the seeds, each of which has a papery wing to assist in wind dispersal. To prevent this happening, encase the pod in a paper or mesh bag attached to the tree. Leave the pod on the tree as long as possible to allow the seeds to ripen (until the pod splits and releases the seeds).

Step 2

Pods can contain up to 100 seeds. They can remain viable for up to three years, if kept under cool, dry and dark conditions in paper bags, but are best sown as soon as ripe. They should be creamy white and fleshy when cut.

Step 3

At night prior to sowing, place the seeds between several layers of wet paper towelling overnight to accelerate germination. The seeds that do not swell are probably not viable and are best discarded. Using fresh seeds will increase germination rate.

Step 4

Fill a seedling tray with seed raising mix. Commercial mixes are available, or you can prepare your own—mix two thirds perlite or sand with one third potting mix or peat moss. Vermiculite tends to hold too much moisture. Tamp down the surface with a flat board. Rather than using seed raising trays some enthusiasts sow into individual tubes. Whatever you use, make sure they're well labelled.

Step 5

Thoroughly wet the mix prior to sowing. Sow thinly, that is space the seed well, about 50 millimetres (2 inches) apart, and barely cover them. Insert each seed vertically so that the papery wing sticks up. The papery wings should protrudes above the mix. Pinch the soil around each seed to ensure good contact.

Step 6

In climates away from the tropics, bottom heat is desirable to hurry germination. Do not water again until the soil is almost dry. Use a mist spray bottle to reduce the likelihood of dislodging the seed. If 'damping off' fungus is a problem (wilted seedlings), incorporate a fungicide in the water. Germination should be complete within three to fourteen days. Transplant seedlings into individual pots when they have two or three sets of true leaves. The first set is seed leaves (cotyledons), supplying nourishment to the growing seedling.

Step 7

Young seedlings have brittle root systems and must be handled with great care when transplanting. Watering with dilute (half-strength) fertiliser will encourage a sturdy seedling that grows fast and requires 'potting on' within a very short time to avoid it becoming pot bound. Failure to do this results in encircling roots, which handicap the plant from the start and is a condition from which the tree usually never recovers. Such trees remain weak and always prone to blowing over in strong winds. During establishment a shade house is ideal for protecting seedlings, and morning sun is most beneficial. Pinching the growing tip will encourage branching and, in turn, a sturdy structure.

Step 8

In tropical climates a seedling may reach 900 millimetres (35 inches) at one year of age and even flower, but in cooler climates only 300 millimetres (12 inches) or so can be expected. First-year seedlings are defined as not having gone through a winter. Growth during this year will be enhanced if a fertiliser with a high nitrogen content is blended into the potting mix. Plants grown indoors must be sprayed with a systemic insecticide to protect them against spider mites, mealy bug, white fly etc. During the growing season the seedling should receive six hours of sunshine per day.

Step 9

If the plant survives its first winter, it becomes a second-year seedling, and should be grown in a 200-millimetre (8-inch) pot, using a good quality potting mix and a handful of well-composted manure. Six hours of sun is required for optimum growth.

Step 10

A seedling that survives its second winter has the honour of 'probably' flowering in its third year. Flowering should occur within three years, but may take up to 25 years depending on genetic make-up, climate and growing conditions. Some seedlings may never flower. They will all be extremely variable in flower colour, size and shape, as well as plant habit, which can vary from compact to lanky and willowy. In addition, the first flowers may not be indicative of future performance.

Step 11

If you have created a wonderful new variety and want to keep it, it's up to you to give it a name. A registered name must be unique, two or three words long, and contain the place, person or a description. Or you can give it a number, or designation, that describes where it came from, until you give it a proper name.

Grafting

For frangipani varieties of low vigour, propagation by cuttings can have disappointing results. To overcome this, grafting is a logical method of propagation, with the procedure ideally undertaken towards the end of the dormant period or early spring.

It is best to select a vigorous variety as the understock, that is, the plant that will provide the root system. In the tropics *Plumeria obtusa* is excellent and in cooler climates 'Celadine' is a reliable choice. They must, of course, be healthy plants. As with all grafting, the aim is to achieve the best possible match between the cambium of the understock and the cambium of the 'scion' (the variety one is attempting to propagate).

With the thick wood typical of frangipanis, apical grafting is recommended. But in each technique (see sketches) a scion of a diameter as close as possible to that of the understock is best. Ideally it should be around 300 millimetres (12 inches) long and cut into mature grey bark—green bark material is too young and soft for the procedure.

LEFT: When a stem is grafted it will commonly throw out a new shoot immediately below the graft. Remove this to avoid competition.
RIGHT: Wound sealant is painted on the wound to seal against insects or disease.

In all grafting a sealant, usually sold as 'tree and wound sealant' or 'grafting sealant', is desirable once the graft procedure is completed. Applied as a liquid, it excludes air and moisture from the cut surfaces. Some enthusiasts also mix a fungicide powder with this to create a paste. This will give added protection.

Splice or Whip Graft

The simplest graft is the 'splice' or 'whip graft', which involves making a long, slanting cut at the base of the scion and a corresponding cut towards the apex of the stock. Again this is into mature grey bark wood. When placed together there should be good contact between the cambium layers. The root stock and scion are then carefully bound and sealed together to keep the junction firm and to exclude moisture.

Chisel Graft

In the chisel graft the scion is also ideally about 300 millimetres (12 inches) long and cut into a chisel point using a sharp knife. A corresponding 'V' shape is then made into grey bark of the understock, so that the stock and scion match as closely as possible, with the cambium of each in contact. Using the same diameter wood for each of the parts will encourage this. The junction should then be carefully sealed against moisture. To bind these grafts (both the chisel and the splice), use grafting or budding tape, plastic strip, raffia, cling wrap or similar. Splints of bamboo skewers, split bamboo, etc can be usefully employed around the stems to hold the graft firmly.

Depending upon the climate and weather conditions, a successful 'take', indicated by leaf growth or elongation of the scion tip, may be expected within one to two months. At that point the tape and splints may be carefully removed.

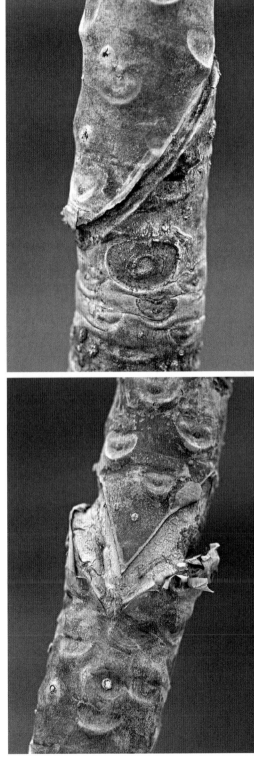

Top: Splice or whip graft.
Below: Chisel graft.

Patch Budding

When propagating material is in short supply, it is possible to use a single bud from the desired variety in a technique known as patch budding. Take a tip cutting from the desired plant and leave it to dry out for a month or so, at which time the buds should have swollen. Then, using a sharp chisel, remove a small square of wood around a bud. Cut through the bark and cambium into the heartwood. Then remove a patch of the same shape and size from an area of grey bark on the receptor plant. Insert the bud patch into this and secure it in place with grafting tape. Be careful to keep the correct bud orientation.

Once the bud starts to grow, usually after a month or so, cut off and discard the stem above the new bud, which then assumes the role of growth leader.

TOP: This tree in the garden owned by enthusiast Fuzzy Moody at Oahu, Hawai'i, has been grafted over a period of 20 years with dozens of varieties. It has been heavily pruned many times and various grafts tested. Nowadays, Fuzzy prefers chisel grafts for their ease and reliability. When in the deciduous condition, close inspection reveals that almost every grafting initiates a new shoot near the cut end from the understock, as well as the scion.
LEFT: A sight to behold, this 100 year old 'Frankenstein' tree has been grafted with over 80 different cultivars. Nong Nooch Tropical Botanic Gardens, Thailand.

Rainbow Trees

As a garden feature, whether the garden be sprawling acres, a small courtyard or simply a balcony of potted plants, what could be more arresting than a frangipani displaying more than one colour of flower? It's easy to achieve and the results are spectacular.

As outlined already, many individual varieties show a range of colours, both within a flower and from one flower to the next on the same tree. But it is also possible—and fun—to graft a tree to several different varieties of *Plumeria rubra*. The basic rules are: start with a healthy and vigorous tree as your understock and select a number of cultivars that have similar vigour of growth and flowering habit. Obviously choose colours to suit your own preference, but also select on the basis of vigour to avoid the more vigorous varieties shading out other grafts. This is a principle long-practised with multi-grafted fruit trees, and if you ignore the advice, you may end up with a tree that requires ongoing selective pruning out of some of the more vigorous growth, or a tree of just one or two varieties. Varieties that have similar flowering 'peaks' also produce the best effects.

Arguably the best understock is the widely grown *Plumeria rubra* var. *acutifolia* because of its hardiness and vigour. It also has a spreading branch habit and yellow/white flowers that become the 'filler' to show off the other coloured forms. But if you are lucky to already possess an established and healthy tree of another variety, there is no reason why you can't set to work on it as the root stock for your rainbow tree.

Another method of achieving a rainbow effect is traditional in some regions and involves planting cuttings of several varieties together in the one hole. If they have been selected for equivalent vigour, in time they will be hard to distinguish from a grafted rainbow tree. Because their root systems are effectively competing with each other, you need to manage your 'tree' carefully, with regular applications of fertiliser and mulching. If it is potted, it will require more water than a similar planting in the ground.

7. Cultivars

If the only available frangipani were 'Celadine', who could ask for more? Certainly many gardeners would be content. But there is a plethora of frangipani varieties to choose from, old and new. Specialist nurseries are burgeoning, numerous websites are devoted to the genus and interest groups proliferate, with the first International Plumeria Convention planned as we write.

Some of the available varieties are cultivars, varieties so designated after rigorous evaluation of desirable, relatively stable characteristics and worthy of being propagated through the nursery trade. The Plumeria Society of America, founded in 1979, administers the recognised register for this. At the time of writing 360 cultivars are described on the register. Of the countless other varieties that remain unregistered, many would be worthy of cultivar status. Not until several specimens of a particular variety have been trialled over a period of at least three years can we be confident that characteristics are relatively stable. Only then may the variety be considered for registration; 'reversions' to a different form are not uncommon in many groups of plants.

To perpetuate a cultivar it is essential that propagation be by vegetative means, that is by cuttings, grafting or tissue culture. This ensures identical genetic make-up is passed to the progeny. Seedlings from a cultivar have different genetic make-up and therefore are not the same variety. Even though many seedlings will tend to reflect characteristics of the known parent tree, the pollen parent usually remains a mystery.

LEFT: 'Capalaba Pink', Tweed Heads, Australia.

'Celadine'

'Celadine' is the most widely grown, hardiest and arguably most admired of all frangipanis. Registration number 191 in the *2006 Register of Cultivars*, 'Celadine' is described as: 'brilliant yellow, with a broad white margin around the petal; narrow petals, pointed tip, slightly overlapping, good texture; 3.5 inches (90 millimetres) in diameter; strong lemon fragrance; keeping quality very good.'

Enthusiasts, including the Eggenbergers, who wrote the *Handbook on Plumeria Culture*, hold that many 'strains' of this cultivar are found varying in flower size, with varying extents of the white margin around its firm-textured petals, but they always have the delicious and distinctive fragrance and exceptional keeping quality.

The 'brilliant yellow' is the clue to the name of this universally popular cultivar. After extensive research we have concluded that its name was almost certainly inspired by the colour resemblance to several plant species known variously as Celandine, Celandine Poppy and Celadine Poppy.

The first-century Roman naturalist Pliny mentions in his writings the True Celandine (*Chelidonium majus*), an herbaceous perennial in the family Papaveraceae widespread throughout Eurasia. Its botanical name derives from the Greek name, *chelidon*, for the migratory swallow, the bird sometimes called the Harbinger of Spring. Reputedly when the swallows arrive, the brilliant yellow flowers appear. True Celandine is also known as Swallow Wort and Greater Celandine, to distinguish it from the Lesser Celandine (*Ranunculus ficaria*), another brilliant yellow flowered herb from the Mediterranean. A tuberous perennial, True Celandine has long been used medicinally in China and is one of the plant species the botanist John Tradescant the Younger grew in his London garden around 1656.

Yet another species, *Stylophorum diphyllum* from eastern North America, is commonly known as Celadine Poppy and Wood Poppy. A yellow-flowered medicinal herb in the family Papaveraceae is used as treatment for skin and eye disorders as well as a dye. Another member of this family from tropical America, *Bocconia frutescens*, is known as Tree Celandine. Reaching around 6 metres (20 feet) in height, it is a vigorous species, seeding and suckering prolifically. In Hawai'i it is considered a noxious weed and the stem when cut exudes a brilliant yellow sap.

OPPOSITE: *Plumeria rubra* var. *acutifolia* 'Celadine' in all its glory.

Bill Moragne Hybrids

Born in Hilo, Hawai'i, in 1905 and a civil engineering graduate of the University of Hawai'i, William Moragne Snr worked in the sugar industry as manager of Grove Farm Plantation on the island of Kauai. A passionate plantsman, he is credited with having produced the first controlled frangipani hybridisations after experimenting over a 20-year period and recording his results in the 1950s.

As the pollen parent and seed parent, respectively, Moragne used: 'Scott Pratt' (also called 'Kohala Red'), which possesses small red flowers and a slight spicy fragrance; and 'Daisy Wilcox', which is technically described as a white, because that is the principal colour, but actually has large pale pink flowers that quickly fade to white with a prominent yellow centre, strong pink bands on the petal reverse, and a spicy fragrance. After some trial and error, he skilfully performed the crosspollination. Upon successful fertilisation four seed pods developed and were collected. From these he propagated a remarkable
283 seedlings. Many of these he grew to maturity—some plants taking up to 18 years to flower—and from the huge diversity of flower forms and colours, and plant habits, ranging from leggy to compact, he selected his favourites and named them after the female members of his family. These he planted around his home. These cultivars have now been placed on The Plumeria

Descriptions

'Jean Moragne': syn. 'Jean Moragne Snr' was named after William Moragne's wife. Described as cerise fading to pale pink at the edges, with a red centre and strong rose fragrance.

'Jeannie Moragne': syn. 'Jean Moragne Jnr' after his daughter-in-law. Described as red fading to reddish pink with strong yellow bands and pink/orange lines radiating outwards and a strong fragrance.

'Mary Moragne': after his daughter. Described as pale creamy pink with a golden orange centre and spicy fragrance.

'Sally Moragne': after another daughter. Described as light peach pink fading to white and pink at the edges, with a golden centre, prominent red veining and strong sweet fragrance.

'Cyndi Moragne': after a granddaughter. Described as creamy white with a large bright yellow centre and slight fragrance.

Society of America's *Registration List*. He planted other selected forms along the highway that once led into Grove Farm. The diversity of these selections is truly fascinating, even including significant yellows (see the Family Tree on next page). Sadly a combination of neglect, a hurricane in 1982, the theft of cuttings and the fact that the trees were apparently planted in 44-gallon (170-litre) drums, causing root girdling, have taken their toll.

Unfortunately, Moragne's records of his experimentation and trials have never been found, but details of his technical skills have been handed down by family and friends, so that his name continues to be remembered—the cultivar 'Bill Moragne' has been registered, but is yet to be allocated to a deserving recipient. As an interesting aside, Moragne actually called 'Daisy Wilcox', 'Grove Farm', but that name has subsequently been registered for a totally different cultivar.

ABOVE: Grove Farm homestead, built in 1864, sits serenely in a majestic landscape of mature trees. Here Bill Moragne Snr was manager of the sugarcane plantation from 1928–69. Today the property is managed as a 'Living Museum' and guided tours are available.

'Katie Moragne': after another daughter. Described as vibrant brick-red contrasting with soft white of the rolled inner edge of each petal, with a yellow centre and strong, sweet fragrance. Described by Eggenberger as the most striking and intensely coloured of the Moragne hybrids.

'Kimi Moragne': after a granddaughter. Described as intense rose pink fading to light pink at the extreme edge, with an orange centre and sweet fragrance akin to the carnation *Dianthus* sp.

'Julie Moragne': after a granddaughter. Described as white with a gold throat and red eye and a bright crimson band on one edge of the petal underside.

'Edi Moragne': after a granddaughter. Described as white with medium gold throat and gold eye, white reverse and strong jasmine fragrance.

'Kelly Moragne': after a granddaughter. Description not available at time of writing.

The Moragne Family Tree

Parent: 'Scott Pratt'

Selected and named offspring:

'Jean Moragne'   'Jeannie Moragne'.   'Mary Moragne'   'Sally Moragne'

Rejected and unnamed offspring:

Parent: 'Daisy Wilcox'

'Katie Moragne'   'Cyndi Moragne'   'Kimi Moragne'   'Julie Moragne'   'Edi Moragne'

Jim Little Hybrids

Shortly before Jim Moragne's death, he passed his tricks of the trade and pollination secrets down to Mr Jim Little, another plumeria enthusiast in Hawai'i. Jim Little became the world's next best breeder and is world renowned for quality cultivars produced as mail-order cuttings. He now runs a large plumeria mail-order nursery with his family in Hawai'i.

Among Little's contributions to the world of plumeria is 'Donald Angus Red', a cross made by the University of Hawai'i, named by Little and horticulturist Richard Criley in honour of Little's friend and mentor, who taught Little much of what he knows. Little records that Angus collected plants from all over the world and donated many to the Foster Botanic Gardens in Honolulu.

On a collecting trip to Malaysia, Little brought back 15 plumeria cuttings, including a double-flowered one called 'Bali Whirl' and another with peach-coloured flowers called 'Penang Peach'. Both have now become internationally recognised and beloved varieties. Another of his great finds was 'Theresa Wilder' which:

'Theresa Wilder'.

'*...came to my attention last summer when a landscape colleague of mine asked me to trim a tree for him. It turned out to be this plumeria that I first heard of in 1975, but is hard to find now. Kauka Wilder, an associate in botany at the Bishop Museum, named the flower. He named it for his sister-in-law. The flowers are a pinwheel rainbow of orange to pink and coral. It has good colour intensity and I recommend it for landscaping.*'

Jim Little

Hawaiian Favourites

'Jim Little Pink Pansy': cleanly marked pink and white blooms shaped like pansies. Red edge on back. Good, sweet fragrance. Compact. Unusual.

'J.L. Starlight': 1994 introduction with huge 10-cm (4-inch) flowers, white with yellow centre and a red band on petal rim and reverse. Sweet perfume scent.

'J.L. Hawaiian Titanic': each large 14-cm (6-inch) flower has a delicate pink band on one side and a small yellow throat and cute notched petal tip. Fragrant.

'J.L. Hawaiian Sunset': a streaking white vein of rainbow colours radiating from a 10-cm (4-inch) vivid pink flower. The white veins are also visible on the reverse side of the flower. The petals are ovate and slightly overlapped. Flowers have a mild sweet fragrance. A seedling from 'Kimi Moragne'.

'J.L. Bridal White': a small brilliant white flower with small lemon-yellow eye. Good fragrance. Compact grower.

'J.L. Trumpet': a small brilliant white flower with small lemon yellow eye. Good fragrance. Compact grower.

'J.L. Church Ruffles': Large 10-cm (4-inch) pinkish white flower with a deep orange eye. Slightly curled and ruffled petals with excellent strong sweet fragrance. Dark green foliage and rounded form.

LEFT: 'Donald Angus Red'.
TOP RIGHT: 'J. L. Trumpet.'
BELOW RIGHT: 'J. L. Pink Pansy'.

Steven Prowse Collection

Many of Australia's frangipani enthusiasts live in tropical north Queensland and some have established nurseries there. Steven Prowse, of Sacred Garden Frangipanis, Mount Garnet, lists an extensive cultivar range including cultivars he has collected throughout his remote area of northern Australia. 'Garnet Gem' was recently discovered as a wild seedling in the state's Gulf country. 'Harlequin', an unusual seedling tree, was discovered in Cape York.

In the late nineteenth and early twentieth centuries in Australia's top end, Polynesian Christian missionaries, coming mainly from Samoa and Vanuatu, established mission settlements for the local Aborigines. They brought with them their favourite sacred frangipanis for planting around the missions. Although the missions were finally abandoned, old mango trees, coconut palms and frangipanis have survived, despite the cyclones, prolonged droughts and frequent fires that are characteristic of dry savannah bushland. The cultivars 'Queen Napranum' and 'King Napranum' were both discovered growing wild at an abandoned Samoan-run mission site in the Gulf country.

Cuttings from these trees, as well as self-sown seedlings, have provided ample breeding stock, and these are now being combined with exciting varieties from other countries such as Thailand. This, in turn has led to cultivars such as 'Sacred Garden Grace' and 'Aiden Prowse', world-class cultivars with drought resistance and incredible vigour.

TOP LEFT TO RIGHT: 'Mayan Gold', 'Queen Napranum', 'Garnet Gem', 'Flame', and 'North Queensland Blue.'

BELOW LEFT TO RIGHT: 'Salsa', 'Sacred Garden Pink Lily', Harlequin', 'Sacred Garden Grace', and ' Blood Red'.

Aussie Favourites

Pictured left:

'Mayan Gold' is a world-class deep gold and the darkest golden yellow of all Australian cultivars. It was discovered in north Queensland as a single old seedling tree. The pure yellow flower emerges a deep golden yellow, fading to pure butter yellow. The back of the flower is yellow and pink.

'Queen Napranum', a soft tricolor of white, pink and lemon.

'Garnet Gem' has large, richly fragrant cerise pink blooms and was recently discovered as a wild seedling in Queensland's remote Gulf country.

'Flame' is a seedling from 'Janet's Ginger'. It has a pure orange flame colour.

'Moonlight Pink' is pure baby pink on front and back. The large flower has a beautiful shape. The unusually textured petals resemble pink crepe paper.

'North Queensland Blue' is a rare and beautiful lilac/lavender discovered in north Queensland.

'Salsa' is an unusual pink-grey with a dark eye.

'Sacred Garden Pink Lily' is a rare interspecific hybrid of *Plumeria rubra* and *P. pudica*. It is a beautiful hybrid of Steven's breeding. The flowers have a beautiful shape and colour—pastel pink and white with a rare golden yellow and red centre. The lovely shaped foliage is semi-deciduous or evergreen.

'Harlequin' has unusual thin candy pink petals with a yellow eye and white blush. This beautiful seedling tree was discovered in remote Cape York.

'Sacred Garden Grace' has large pure white overlapping round petals with a small yellow eye.

'Blood Red' is now sometimes called 'Black Red' or 'Suva Red'. It was brought into Australia many years ago, probably by Christian missionaries from Polynesia who brought many frangipani varieties with them when they established new missions in the Torres Strait Islands and then mainland Australia. It has a spicy fragrance.

Other varieties:

'Aiden Prowse' has strong smoked-salmon petals with hot pink tips, and glossy disease-resistant clean foliage. Prowse named this cultivar after his son and he considers it a unique world-class cultivar.

'Cooktown Queen' syn. 'Wishy Washy' has huge blooms that fade significantly in sunlight.

'Firedancer' is a truly exceptional frangipani with intense colour. The flower is large and the perfume is one of the richest and sweetest of all the frangipani perfumes.

'Sacred Garden Giant' has huge flowers 12 centimetres (5 inches) across. It is the biggest of the fruit salad types, with rich darker colours and broader petals.

'Sacred Garden Sunray' is one of the latest releases, a seedling of 'Weipa Sunset' with large flowers with strong red venation radiating out from centre.

Future Frangipanis

For frangipani fanatics, the future holds great promise and many fascinating surprises. We can expect to see an increasing range of interspecific hybrids (hybrids created by crossing two species of plumeria) and more variegated foliages. Thousands of new cultivars are being produced in countries such as Thailand, with growers visiting these breeders every year, bringing home their choices to be checked in quarantine stations, grown in open paddocks and tested for home gardeners before being released onto the market. Wait until these new varieties are proven before giving one pride of place in your garden, as each cultivar will respond differently to different soils, temperatures and other environmental factors.

Little-known species such as *Plumeria pudica*, and particularly one labelled 'Everlasting Love', will become more common as the general public realise their potential in warm, subtropical and tropical climates. These plants will become better known for their hedging properties, growing to 3 metres in full sun, they are drought tolerant and have interesting hammerhead-shaped leaves.

Top: Grafting has become big business in Thailand. Here just-grafted plants wait on benches for the graft to 'take'.
Below: Tissue culture in Thailand.

Interspecific Hybrids

The cultivar 'Dwarf Singapore' is reputedly a hybrid between *Plumeria obtusa* 'Singapore' and *Plumeria rubra* 'King Kalakaua'. But, as with many so-called dwarf cultivars, in time they can reach substantial size, up to 2 metres (6 feet). The cultivar 'Mele Pa Bowman' also known as 'Evergreen Singapore Yellow' is known to be a hybrid between *Plumeria obtusa* 'Singapore' and *Plumeria rubra* var. *acutifolia*.

Tissue Culture

One way to produce an exact copy of a plant from its own cells is to clone it through a process called tissue culture, stem culture or tip culture. Research teams admit that commercially this kind of propagation cannot yield the viable return of investment and time compared with the grafting or budding methods. But propagators hope that one day it will be a viable solution. In practice, the procedures require consistency in the steps of tip selection, sterilisation, tools and temperature control, with an 80 per cent success rate considered satisfactory.

Rising Stars of Thailand

Thailand is leading the world with modern cultivars, growing exponentially with the new methods of propagation such as grafting and budding—6000 new varieties this year alone. Thousands of these new locally bred hybrids are slowly trickling into the world's markets from nurseries such as Jack's, Danney's, Edi's, Nok's and Widget. Over time they will become more and more available to home gardeners. Variegated foliages are becoming more available, although the jury is still out as to whether they will become popular on world markets.

TOP, LEFT TO RIGHT: 'Jack's Purple' syn 'Violet Princess', 'Elsie', and 'Orange Special'.
BELOW, LEFT TO RIGHT: 'Dwarf Orange', 'Tornado', and 'Anyamanee' (with variegated foliage).

Named Cultivars

There are thousands of 'named' hybrid frangipani flowers on the market. Following is a small selection of proven performers you'll be able to find in specialist nurseries. These are readily available cultivars with exceptional flowering ability. The extent of their colour, size, variety, shape, texture and perfume is breathtaking, making a decision difficult, if not impossible!

1. 'Celadine'
2. 'Bali Whirl'
3. 'Elena'
4. 'King Kalakaua'
5. 'Gardenia'
6. 'Samoan Fluff'
7. 'Hausten White'
8. 'Petite Pink'
9. 'Ramona'
10. 'Bowen Yellow'
11. 'Paul Weissich'
12. 'Heidi'

13. 'Nebel's Gold'
14. 'Nebel's Rainbow'
15. 'Edi Moragne'
16. 'Cyndi Moragne'
17. 'Yellow Gold'
18. 'Kimo'
19. 'Apricot Tricolor'
20. 'White Shell'
21. 'J. L. Pink Pansy'
22. 'India'
23. 'Daisy Wilcox'
24. 'Tillie Hughes'

25. 'Madame Poni'
26. 'Pauahi Ali'
27. 'Jeannie Moragne'
28. 'Maui Beauty'
29. 'Puu Kahea'
30. 'Kanehoe Sunburst'
31. 'Moragne Seedling No. 9'
32. 'Loretta'
33. 'Aussie Pink'
34. 'Sharna's Pink'
35. 'Kirra Dawn'
36. 'Grove Farm'

37. 'Keiki'
38. 'Katie Moragne'
39. 'Tomlinson'
40. 'Ruffles'
41. 'Julie Moragne'
42. 'Cooktown Sunset'
43. 'Theresa Wilder'
44. 'Sharna's Rose'
45. 'Pink Cherry'

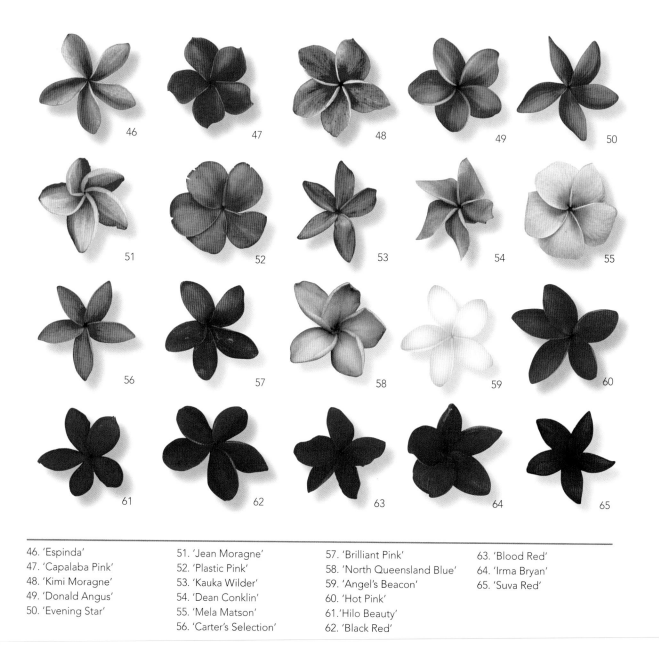

46. 'Espinda'
47. 'Capalaba Pink'
48. 'Kimi Moragne'
49. 'Donald Angus'
50. 'Evening Star'

51. 'Jean Moragne'
52. 'Plastic Pink'
53. 'Kauka Wilder'
54. 'Dean Conklin'
55. 'Mela Matson'
56. 'Carter's Selection'

57. 'Brilliant Pink'
58. 'North Queensland Blue'
59. 'Angel's Beacon'
60. 'Hot Pink'
61. 'Hilo Beauty'
62. 'Black Red'

63. 'Blood Red'
64. 'Irma Bryan'
65. 'Suva Red'

Duplication in Naming

The difficulty in accurately identifying varieties is demonstrated well by a striking and distinctive variety with long, narrow, twisted incurving and upturned petals, which suffers from the common disadvantage of being called different names in different regions. On the *2004 Registration List*, it is called 'Madame Poni'. But it is also known as 'Ponytail', 'Star', 'Waianae Beauty', 'Corkscrew' and 'Curly Holt'. For a less distinctive variety, the possibility of multiple-naming is magnified many times over and when superficially similar varieties are confused the problem is compounded.

'Madame Poni'.

What Variety Is That?

It is in the nature of the human spirit to want to compare, label, categorise and pigeonhole. This helps us to cope with our complex world in the belief, albeit mistakenly, that we know it. In particular the novice of any discipline seeks definition and labelling as a precursor to 'understanding'.

In the horticultural world, once the genus of a plant is known we can usually quickly conjure up a picture in the mind. Many gardeners can do the same for species. The satisfying aspect of this is that we have in our mind's eye a picture of its cultural requirements—often also its country of origin, natural habitat, potential under cultivation and even its relationships with other species. But since plant hybridisers got to work and new varieties of any species started to be released on the unwary public, it has become a very different story. A plant's 'trade name'—usually something catchy to seduce buyers—often tells us little about the plant. Even when we do see the label, it is not uncommon to find that the parentage of the plant is not revealed, so we have the immediate disadvantage of ignorance of native habitat.

We have to depend wholly on what the label tells us and not until we actually grow this new progeny can we really know its characteristics. This, of course, may lead to surprises, some quite unexpected and some disappointing.

Much depends on what the hybridist was seeking. More often than not it is a showy flower, of large size and vibrant colour, and this is probably the reason we bought the plant. Extended flowering seasons are another common goal. But to meet these objectives, less obvious characteristics are often neglected by the hybridist. For example, in the rose world when Modern Large-flowered roses (sometimes referred to as Hybrid Teas) were being developed with gusto, perfume and disease resistance was almost overlooked. Not until the David Austin releases were these characteristics given the attention they deserve, and of course the disillusioned buying public enthusiastically welcomed the new hybrids in the knowledge that the rose not only had staying power, but also smelt like a rose should smell.

To justify a release being labelled as a new variety, it has to be significantly different to everything that has come before it. With genetically unstable species, that is those that have a propensity to seedling variation, this is a major obstacle. *Camellia japonica* and *Acer palmatum* are such species and also *Plumeria rubra*. When different names are given to perhaps identical or similar varieties that arose as seedling variants in different localities, the picture becomes very confused indeed. 'Madame Poni' demonstrates this (see Duplication in Naming on page 125).

We want to name the plant, we have a strong need to be confident it is such and such, but nature thinks otherwise. Is it not sufficient to simply accept it for the beautiful creation it is and rejoice in this, especially knowing that many frangis are mutable subjects in different climates, under different growing conditions and at different times within the flowering cycle? This approach will never satisfy many enthusiasts, let alone the nursery trade, for whom labelling is integral to their operation. It is also not the way of the horticultural world today. The *2004 Annual Report of the Agricultural Research Service* arm of the US Department of Agriculture said: 'The Ornamentals Industry is continually in need of novel material to maintain consumer interest and industry viability.'

At that time, 86 *Plumeria* cultivars from the Caribbean region had been genotyped and had germplasm collected in a 'microsatellite DNA library' for future research. The Plumeria Society of America supported this work, which will allow a thorough survey of genetic variation and an understanding of the relationships among the cultivars. A plan is also underway to investigate exchange and collection in Thailand.

In making selections from the frangipani feast of cultivars, it is easy to get carried away in thinking only about the glorious flowers. Each has a flowering seasonal peak—early, mid or late. But always when selecting plants for a garden we should consider the whole plant. This includes its overall habit, the way it holds its branches and the nature of branching: Are the stems robust or are they thin and prone to dieback? Is the foliage dark green, dense and healthy or does it tends to be paler and perhaps prone to disfiguration? Is it especially susceptible to the curse of plumeria rust? The gardener must rely on reputation and observation. How will the variety perform under *your* conditions? If you don't know of a specimen in a nearby garden, it is very much a case of 'try and see'.

Current frangipani research pays attention to many factors apart from attractive/eye-catching flowers. 'Compact' growth habits, good substance suitable for lei making, rust resistance and extended flowering periods are just some of these objectives.

Design

8. Use in Design

Frangipanis are the ballerinas, the contortionists and the juggling acts of tropical garden design. Easy to move at almost any size, they are also a garden designer's best friend.

Made Wijaya

From the perspective of garden design, the frangipani suits many styles, while offering the ideal scale and proportion. They have been used throughout the world in high-end resort landscaping, collected in botanic gardens, used in public parks, along avenues or at the beach, and grown at home. Frangipanis are the perfect size for us to feel comfortable under their branches—not too big, not too small, but just right. They fit with us and us with them.

Made Wijaya, a landscape designer who inspired a tropical garden revolution with his romantic 'new Balinese' style, believes that, 'frangipanis are the most widely used tree in the tropics'. The vast number of frangipani cultivars makes Wijaya's statement even more plausible today, where recent breeding and selection has resulted in countless new varieties from all areas of the world. This small tree has become an icon of the tropics; its curvaceous shape is appreciated for its sculptural qualities. Australian artist and long-time Balinese resident Donald Friend, who painted frangipanis in his work *Batujimbar Village*, said, 'the torso of the frangipani is the tropical world's oak'. Dramatic effects can be achieved both in gardens and paintings by playing on their reef-like silhouette.

The frangipani is a plant of rare beauty and has something different to offer, no matter the season. In winter its skeletal branches stand out from the

crowd, allowing the sun to come streaming in to warm the garden below. In spring its new cloak of lush foliage speaks of renewal. In summer its strong form helps to draw attention to the garden ceiling and provide dazzling floral colour, while shading us from the heat of the summer sunshine. Flowers and fragrance persist into autumn in most areas.

While they can be left unpruned, with a bit of imagination, inspiration and some lessons in judicious pruning, frangipanis can be not only an essential element of tropical and subtropical gardens, but the star attraction. This small tree throws a large shadow, giving welcome shade. Their simple flowers and fragrance evoke vivid memories of tropical holidays. Potted on a deck, patio or balcony or planted as a small tree in the garden, they are resilient and reliable. Frangipanis perform no matter where they're situated. They are wonderful lit up at night, and their flowers make beautiful decorations in float bowls around the home, or can even decorate the body, as in leis. There is little limit to their application, and if you've fallen in love with them, here are some fabulous ways you can enjoy them in your own home.

PREVIOUS PAGE: Frangipanis are a big part of tropical garden design. Four Seasons Resort, Jimbarin Bay, Bali.

ABOVE: Frangipanis have the ideal scale.

Opposite: This backyard tree is relished for its shade and fragrance. It's a wonderful way to celebrate summer, the holiday season and dining outdoors. Sydney, Australia

Above: A wayward trunk is sympathetically accommodated by this picket fence, becoming part of the streetscape. Sydney, Australia.

Left: Past the shapely trunk of this tree the eye is drawn to the Pacific Ocean, NSW South Coast, Australia.

Welcome Home

In Australia frangipanis became fashionable during the nineteenth century, where they adorned Victorian terraces, Federation bungalows and suburban homes. Traditionally they were given top billing, wedged between the house entry and the garden, very close to the house—the perfect position to be greeted with their fragrance.

Houses can cause problems for most plants. While not many trees enjoy a restricted root space, frangipanis flourish in tight positions, crammed into a small root run next to building foundations. Shade and reflected heat can play havoc, dramatically changing the microclimate, but frangipanis cope with both.

When frangipanis are planted close to buildings or feature walls, they provide what landscape architects call 'vertical relief'. Their trunks and branches have a strong sculptural form, which breaks up a solid wall or structure, creating wonderful shadows in living areas and open verandas. The

A blue picket fence and gate with twin frangipanis creates a boundary between the public nature of the street and the privacy of the home. As soon as you enter through the gate there is peace and quiet. Freshwater, Australia.

frangipani is also the ideal height to bring the size of a house into comfortable scale for the rest of the garden. One drawback of planting close to the house, however, is that the trees are unable to spread their canopy fully.

In terms of creating a passive solar home, frangipanis are top of the list. Planted on the hot side of a house, they can provide direct relief from soaring summer temperatures. During winter, when they are deciduous, they let the warmth into the house. Plant frangipanis where you can also enjoy them from inside, perhaps from a balcony, a second-storey window or veranda—a bird's eye view of these trees is breathtaking on a balmy summer evening.

A front garden offers a welcoming presence to the street, as well as providing an attractive outlook from the house. Frangipani can be planted along a front fence to screen views to the street, or you could plant them either side of the front gate to create an arc of branches to encourage visitors in or to frame the vista beyond.

Give a frangipani the room to spread, and you will be rewarded with a unique feature tree. Judicious pruning can result in a tree with faultless proportions, a trunk in harmony with its branches and a mushroom-cloud canopy perfectly balanced with its shadow. The canopy needs ample air space to develop—at least 5 metres (16 feet) of uninterrupted freedom—so frangipanis make excellent focal points. Their sculptural branches and distinctive outline help them to stand apart from other planting. Leaving the frangipani free of other planting can further enhance its profile. This also allows views of the trunk, which often becomes gnarled, contorted with age and covered in silvery sheen with lichen and moss. In a lawn or simple patterned paving, the tree casts beautiful shadows. A verdant lawn also accentuates not only the tree's beauty and form, but also the circles of colourful petals that fall.

Alternatively, try clump planting, a technique in which frangipanis are planted in small groves to look like a natural forest. Try planting different colours in an odd-numbered patch, with a swathe of one ground cover beneath. This results in a sensational series of trunks, canopies that blend into each other and a uniform understorey. Odd numbers help to achieve a balanced composition or picture. Trim trees heavily to encourage shapely branches and thin canopies to develop a sculptural form. Plant the trees at least 2 metres (6 feet) away from each other to best create this effect.

Around the Home

The back garden is usually a private area and should be designed for maximum relaxation, privacy, entertaining and practicalities. In large gardens, the subtropical and tropical style relies on sweeping, curved garden beds with abundant flowers and foliage and expanses of lush lawn. Where space permits, an outdoor pavilion, hammock, lily pond or garden seat can be designed alongside a feature frangipani. Back gardens trap the fragrance of frangipani, which is beneficial to outdoor entertaining areas. Frangipanis are also excellent for creating much-needed shade in summer. Grown beside or through a deck, just one tree will be sufficient to create the perfect low maintenance retreat.

A striking tree provides the focal point to this garden; its lifted canopy permits underplanting, giving interest at ground level.

Public Spaces

Frangipanis make admirable street trees for public spaces, shopping malls, road verges and car parks. They are ideal for planting under electrical wires as they will rarely need the 'crown reduction' other trees endure and if they do, they respond well. Rarely requiring watering, they are a good option for a neglected street verge. They flower reliably each year despite paving up to their trunks, and they need little attention but give glorious shade for pedestrians and parked cars in summer. The perfect avenue is achieved when trees are planted 4 metres (13 feet) apart.

Frangipanis in public places will nearly always need to be 'crown lifted'. Crown lifting is the gradual removal of the lowest branches over time. This has the added benefit of giving a regular height from ground level to create a uniform avenue of trees. It gives councils the opportunity to plant them as street trees and in car parks.

Evergreen varieties such as *Plumeria pudica* and *Plumeria stenophylla* hold much promise in tropical areas. As they don't shed their leaves in the tropics, they are a tidy option for suburban streets. They are also excellent for providing year-round shade in car parks and for reducing 'glare' from extensive paving. Spreading canopies trap wind-blown dust and filter the air of urban environments. And all plumeria species, but especially those with glossy leaves, have extreme tolerance to air pollution—a reality of life in urban environments.

Plumeria obtusa, planted in raised planter boxes at Oasis shopping centre, Broadbeach, Australia. In this hot climate evergreens are especially appreciated.

Water Gardens

Water is a heavenly combination with the frangipani, creating reflections, shade and cool air. Place a frangipani gently arching over a pond, with a well-placed urn or pot to nuzzle into the trunk, and its branches will lightly frame views of the pond.

Excellent examples of this friendship between elements exist in Bali and Thailand. Made Wijaya's Bali compound at Villa Bebek, Sanur, with over 20 different water features within its walls, is a superb case in point. Here water and frangipani exist in harmony with each other; delicate frangipani shadows play on the surface of the water. In this garden, water is life. Still water, gently running water, spilling water, falls, dribbles and splashes bring excitement and life into the courtyards. Not only does the water provide relaxation, but refuge for wildlife too, and frogs, fish and tadpoles are at home here. The pond edges are simple stone, rock or pebbles, and many boundaries are disguised with spilling foliages such as bromeliads, russelia or ferns. Water lilies and lotus are

The formal pool of the walled courtyard garden is graced with a central tree incorporated into the modern water feature. Its graceful trunk is accentuated through sensitive pruning. Reflections and fallen flowers are a bonus.

two sacred flowering aquatic plants suitable for ponds, and these flower at the same time as your frangipani.

Not all of us are blessed with a large garden which can encompass a large-scale water feature, and most of us must be content with a smaller vignette or scene. Small spaces can be greatly enhanced with water on a small scale. The same elements are required: water, foliage and an overhanging frangipani. Choose a decent sized water pot, water lily and potted frangipani to create a miniature garden, suitable for a sunny balcony, veranda or roof garden.

BELOW LEFT: Floating flowers enhance water lilies that need sunshine for several hours each day—a perfect combination.

BELOW RIGHT: This shallow pebble-filled pond has been designed with four 'island' plantings of a single tree in each corner. The planter box seems to float on the water and the branches generate reflections that play on the surface where its flowers float. The leafy shadow integrates into the ripple of the water's surface. On smaller raised islands, candles are set in a grid pattern for a dramatic nocturnal effect. Nusa Dua Beach Hotel, Bali.

Courtyards

Frangipanis make an eye-catching feature in courtyards. They look good alone, due to the sculptural nature of their trunk and branches. Uncomplicated garden and planting designs accentuate their silhouette, profile, texture and that important extra dimension—their shadow. The shadow effect is particularly relevant in today's contemporary courtyards. Too often a designer, spoilt for choice, will 'over-design' a courtyard with a complex palette of materials, confusing the eye and resulting in a busy space. Simplify the hard landscaping materials to display the intrinsic nature of the frangipani and allow it to create a patchwork of light-dappled shadows.

When designing a courtyard, think about what type of paving you would like. Paving is often necessary in small spaces; it's easy to maintain and adds a decorative element to the ground plane. A combination of large paving slabs of stone or concrete and pebbles works well in areas of high rainfall, as the pebbles provide soak zones. Choose a paving treatment that matches other materials of the house, veranda and the character of the garden.

LEFT: Courtyard shadows provide intricate interest—a sometimes forgotten aspect of garden design. Nusa Dua Beach Hotel, Bali.

OPPOSITE: This courtyard, designed by Australian architect, Glenn Murcutt, needs nothing more than a single frangipani. Simple paving accentuates the shadow patterns proving that less is more. Sydney, Australia.

Lighting

Lighting has become an essential element of the modern garden, and highlighting the tortured branches of a frangipani will enhance the magic of your frangipani long into the night. Adding light creates a new garden, one that's quite different to that seen during the day.

Ensure your yard is lit with the correct mix of accent and focal illumination. There are three choices when it comes to lighting a frangipani: downlighting, uplighting or fairy lighting.

Downlighting imitates natural light and increases safety. It is effective in lighting an outdoor entertaining area from within the canopy of a frangipani and for casting interesting shadows from the canopy onto the floor below. Try not to position the source of the light so it can be seen, as it could dazzle your dinner guests; better to disguise it within the canopy. There is an array of lamp designs one can hang within the canopy to suit the style of your garden.

Uplighting illuminates from the ground up and is often used to light mature frangipanis with their gnarled trunks and branches. Uplighting creates a focal point, beautifies an area and creates shadows and patterns of light. Illuminating the branches and projecting their silhouette onto a wall gives a dramatic feel. A light source from behind the tree reveals the natural beauty within the tracery of limbs.

Fairy lights or LEDs (light emitting diodes) can be tied or wound around the branches to highlight the shape of the branches and extent of the canopy. LEDs provide hundreds of thousands of hours of life with low voltage, low energy consumption and no heat. They are practical and cost-effective systems to run, as they are virtually maintenance free.

The best advice when lighting outdoors is to use quality fittings that will last a lifetime. Determine how much lighting the garden needs and choose the right fixture—interesting results can be achieved with lanterns, hanging lights, solar lights, path lights or floodlights.

Privacy, Screens and Hedging

Enclose your garden in perfume with a row of frangipanis. Imagine a curtain of flowers, all colours of the rainbow, between you and your neighbour. Frangipanis are a good height as a boundary divider between homes, not growing too big to create neighbourly disputes. A mature frangipani will grow just high enough to screen a two-storey house. Plant trees at 4-metre (13-foot) centres to create a continuous screen. Planting an evergreen hedge beneath the trees will create a line and give you more greenery during winter when the frangipani trunks are bare. We have also seen excellent hedges of frangipanis combined with hibiscus, raphis palm, clipped casuarina and *Ixora chinensis*.

Don't ignore vantage points like second-storey windows or verandas and raised decks; they are perfect places to look down over clouds of flowers to really appreciate their colour and fragrance. Trees planted close to the house will

A line of frangipanis in Hawai'i is hedged with a formal row of clipped oleander to ground the screen.

Evergreen *Plumeria stenopylla* is a good choice for a privacy screen that thrives on neglect. Growing to only 2.5 metres (8 feet) it provides a great living fence between neighbours. Mount Coot-tha Botanic Gardens, Brisbane, Australia.

give added privacy to windows. In winter you will be able to see into the heart of the branches, and this is the time for a little branch maintenance. Remove any spongy or rotted branches to increase air circulation through your tree—this will have the added benefit of discouraging fungal disease such as rust and rot.

Alternatively, to keep your privacy in winter and your boundary line looking good, plant evergreen frangipanis, such as *Plumeria stenophylla* and *Plumeria pudica*. These may not yet be readily available in your area, but stock should soon start to reach commercial nurseries. They are an excellent choice for a privacy hedge, as they have an upright form and a deep green cloak of leaves with white flowers.

Pools

People from colder climates usually meet their first frangipani on a tropical holiday, often by the side of the resort pool. The tree's leafy canopy provides welcome shade and respite from the heat, while the divine fragrance makes them the perfect choice for a pool landscape.

Formal pools with equally spaced frangipanis planted along one side help to protect sunbakers from the sun by providing large patches of dense shade. A single large and capacious frangipani beside the pool may be all that is required. Frangipanis are also great growing in pots dotted around a pool if there is no garden space. Heat-loving and heat-resistant, they often grow where nothing else will.

So-called 'jungle pools', made famous by architect Bill Bensley at Wahtilan Lama, Batujimbar, Sanur, and later by Balinese garden designer Made Wijaya, are seductive environments. With planning and engineering, a good designer can crowd a pool with texture, form and colour to create a tropical jungle style. Many pool, pond and garden designers have imitated the work of Wijaya, who calls his gardens 'ordered jungles', and have been inspired by his flair with foliage and ornament, as well as by his love of frangipani. Jungle pools need jungle planting for them to fit into each other. Use plants such as frangipani, philodendron, russelia, ferns, cycads and rhoeo to help to blur the boundaries of the pool edge.

When planting frangipanis by a pool there are a few considerations. Frangipanis should be planted at least 1 metre (3 feet) away from the side of a pool. Although neither deep-rooted nor invasive, it is important the roots have freedom to create an anchor for the tree.

Pool with morning light. The Villas, Seminyak, Bali.

An art in itself is training frangipanis to lean over the pool. A frangipani with the perfect lean seems to hug the pool, creating a roof for the pool, an admirable vignette. Made Wijaya, in *Tropical Garden Design*, mentions he learnt to lean a frangipani from his friend Ketut, and indicates that it might not be as easy as it

seems. It is necessary to train your tree for a few years to create the perfect angle. Staking helps to stabilise the tree while it is young until it can support its own weight. The angle of inclination is important: too much and you feel the tree will fall over, too little and the effect won't be obvious—a roughly 60-degree angle is suitable. Removal of the lower branches may be needed to make a single trunk. Or you may like the look of multi-trunked specimens.

In the same book Wijaya mentions he learnt how to trim frangipanis into tight shapes from Donald Friend. Pruning is an art that many of us in the West simply don't think of. For most of us a frangipani is a 'set and forget' tree with no pruning requirements. So it's interesting to note that in the tropics, frangipanis are often thinned to open up the canopy, allow light into the floor and views through to the sky. You can create a balanced living sculpture with judicious pruning. This is why many domestic frangipanis look so different to those seen in tropical garden designs, where the art of pruning is alive and well.

To thin a frangipani canopy, selectively remove complete stems and branches to increase light penetration and air movement throughout the crown of a tree. Remove branches that rub or cross another branch. No more than one quarter of the living crown should be removed at a time. If it is necessary to remove more, it should be done over a few years. Crown thinning opens the foliage of a tree, reduces weight on heavy limbs, and helps to retain the tree's natural shape. The volume of the branches to be removed will normally be expressed as a percentage of the whole crown. The thinning of the canopy creates a 'lighter' tree and a different shade pattern. Instead of a heavy full shadow, the shade will be lighter and more delicate. More sunlight will reaching the ground, changing the selection of plants that will thrive beneath the frangipani. Dappled sunlight will allow more flowering plants to grow. Ideally, thinning should be done when the tree is dormant.

Sydney Harbour glistens beyond this lap pool. The frangipani offers the perfect canopy for alfresco relaxation in Point Piper, Sydney, Australia.

Top Tip

Frangipanis are resilient to chlorine and salt-water splash so there is no problem with the draining of pools or overflow. Where a frangipani tree overhangs a pool, it is good to cover the pool during late autumn so leaves are caught before entering the filter system. Dispose of them in the bin and not the compost, so as not to continue the cycle of frangipani rust, if prevalent.

Balconies and Terraces

Potted frangipanis make an excellent focus for a balcony garden. They grow brilliantly in pots and planter boxes (see Pots and Planters on page 74). Frangipanis in containers 'soften' spaces, reduce the severity of a blank wall and give colour, texture and fragrance to an outdoor space. You have two choices of style: plant a solitary frangipani into a large tub, or create a small garden by multi-planting spillover plants into the same pot.

The reasons frangipanis are so suited to container culture are that they are a well-behaved tree with a small root system, respond very well to being root bound, love hard pruning and require much less water than most trees. Smaller cultivars that grow up to 3 metres (10 feet) are best, such as 'Suva Red'. Check with the Plumeria/Frangipani Society in your local area for suitable cultivars. True 'dwarf' varieties such 'Dwarf Singapore Pink' (renamed 'Petite Pink' by Richard Eggenberger), 'Petite White', 'Dwarf Watermelon' and 'Dwarf Richard Criley' all grow to 2 metres (6 feet) or less so are perfect for small containers. We have found 'Petite Pink' required a true subtropical climate and dislikes even the lightest frosts.

For larger trees, choose a substantial pot or container so there is adequate root space to grow a good-sized tree. The width and depth of a half wine barrel is excellent, that is width 640 millimetres x height 400 millimetres (25 x 16 inches). Use a good quality potting mix (with 25 per cent perlite to increase drainage), one with water granules and a controlled release fertiliser included. This will ensure that the plant isn't swamped with wet soil. Keep it on the dry side during autumn and winter or it will drown and rot. In the absence of rain, water once or twice a week during spring, three times a week during summer, and reduce watering during autumn and winter to nil when the tree is dormant.

Long-term container care is important. Once your frangipani is mature, you must root prune every three to five years. Carefully extricate the plant out of the pot, prune up to 150 millimetres (6 inches) off the roots, all around the root ball, and place it back into the pot. Infill with a premium potting mix (see also Pots and Planters on page 74).

Frangipani tubs are ideal for hot spots on a balcony, veranda or roof garden. Group them with other tropicals that enjoy the same conditions—hot sun and dry winters—and limit plants to those that love to grow in pots. Try frangipani with succulents, dwarf bougainvilleas, Brazilian jasmine, portulaca, cordylines

and bromeliads. Mulch pots with small pebbles or stones to add to their visual appeal and ability to retain soil moisture.

Rarely affected by sun or windburn, frangipani can be planted successfully on a roof garden. Rooftops are not easy places to establish a garden. Problems with strong sun and gale-force winds restrict plant choice, and yet frangipanis stand up to both admirably. Sunbaked roof gardens will benefit from the shade of a frangipani and a small water feature to create a peaceful mood. Sunny terraces in hot climates will need the shade of a tree or canopy. As deciduous frangipanis lose their leaves in winter they allow the sunshine to warm up the space. Their resilient and drought-tolerant nature makes them a perfect choice if regular watering cannot be assured. However, regular water is advisable in spring and summer for all containerised plants.

The type of rooftop paving and drainage systems you install are important

Frangipanis are a favourite of courtyard gardeners due to their easy-to-grow nature and reliable flowering. Groupings of striking potted plants welcome users to this private swimming pool. The tall matt black pots are a considered choice to absorb warmth, allow for weeping growth with age, and don't detract from the plants in any way.

BELOW LEFT: *Plumeria pudica* grow well in pots.

CENTRE: Dwarf frangipani, such as this 'Pink 100' syn 'Dwarf Watermelon' grow well in large terracotta tubs. Here they are for sale at Chattachuk markets, Bangkok, Thailand.

RIGHT: Glasshouse potted specimans, Nong Nooch Tropical Botanic Gardens, Thailand.

factors when growing any plants in roof gardens, as water will need to drain safely away and not jeopardise the safety of the building structure. Engineers are sometimes required initially to manage the design of these types of gardens. When choosing pots, constructed planter boxes or lightweight fibreglass pots have obvious benefits over terracotta or ceramic. The pot and planter box size needs to be addressed; mature frangipanis require 500 x 500 millimetres (20 x 20 inches) capacity of planting mix for root spread. Depths shallower than 500 millimetres (20 inches) can be tolerated if there is extra room for root spread. Trees are only at risk of sunburn or windburn if left unwatered and unmulched. Long-term care might include root and canopy pruning every five years. Where the weight of soil on rooftop terraces is a concern, frangipanis may be the ideal choice because of their capacity to thrive in small soil or potting mix volumes.

Bonsai

Bonsai is an inspired choice for frangipanis. Dwarf evergreen species such as 'Dwarf Singapore Pink' and 'Dwarf Singapore White' (syn. *Plumeria obtusa* 'Petite Pink' and 'Petite White') are good for this purpose, although you should be aware that they are not truly evergreen in subtropical or temperate climates. However, they are intensely fragrant. Taking years to grow just 0.5 metres (20 inches) high, these varieties naturally bonsai themselves. We have seen mature specimens only 1.2 metres (4 feet) high. Their half-sized, pinwheel-shaped flowers suit the miniature scale of the bonsai. The interesting *Plumeria rubra* 'Dwarf Watermelon' is available but still rare, a strong pink variety with exceptional fragrance.

Choose a low, shallow ceramic pot and a multi-branched plant to create a balanced canopy. Lightly prune the root ball before potting up. Pot up and train your tree, making good use of branch structure. Prune any branches that don't fit with your desired shape. Accept that all bonsai trees require regular watering and are outdoor plants but can be brought indoors for limited periods, where the flowers can be enjoyed at close range.

TOP: Commercial landscapers make excellent use of the 1.5-metre (5-foot) dwarf variety of frangipani called 'Petite Pink'. This has excellent applications for home gardeners whose space is limited. Here it is planted in a planter box and underplanted with a carpet of mondo grass and a few well-placed rocks.

BELOW: *Plumeria obtusa* 'Petite Pink' is suitable for bonsai culture and a good long-term solution for hot spots. This specimen is 10 years old and it stands 0.6 metres (2 feet) high. A black ceramic pot will retain the heat in the root zone, which is important in temperate and subtropical climates.

By the Seaside

Frangipanis relish coastal conditions. They are one of the few small-to-medium trees that thrive in salt-laden air and deep sandy soils. With their ability to withstand sea breezes, they adapt to coastal conditions very well, making them perfect for planting along beach promenades and in front-line coastal gardens. We have spoken to growers on Kauai, Hawai'i, who have had to wipe the salt from the flowers as they pick them for leis in the early morning. The 'Singapore' frangipani (*Plumeria obtusa*) is unsurpassed for front line conditions in tropical environments. In other climates, *Plumeria obtusa/acutifolia* hybrids or varieties are superior along with the benchmark for hardiness, 'Celadine'.

For the last 30 years a frangipani plantation at Smokey Acres Blossoms, Sunset Beach Hawaii, has been producing flowers for lei making. Being in close proximity to the seashore, blooms are often dusted with salt but are otherwise unaffected.

ABOVE: Frangipanis thrive in the Pacific Islands.

LEFT: Exposed to salt laden ocean winds and growing in sandy soils, frangipanis are happy on the seaside. Bingan Beach, Bali.

Frangipane Tart

The frangipani's versatility is honoured in the culinary world. Reputedly invented by Count Cesare Frangipani in Rome in 1532 and taken to Florence the next year, the *Oxford Companion to Food* describes Frangipane as a cream flavoured with almonds.

According to leading Australian restaurateur, Stephanie Alexander, frangipane to a pastry cook is, ' a mixture of ground almonds, butter, sugar and eggs that is sometimes flavoured with a liqueur. It is a quick and delicious filling for a tart'. And that is how you are mostly likely to encounter it: frangipane tart usually comprises a shortcrust pastry flan, half-filled with the above mix and topped with halved stone fruit, such as soaked dried apricots, poached peaches or plums—reminiscent of fallen frangipani flowers perhaps. Almond frangipane is a popular variation of this, with the following recipe from Stephanie. Almond frangipane will keep for a week in a covered container in the refrigerator. It can also be used to fill tartlets.

Ingredients:
shortcrust pastry (piecrust dough)
120 grams (1 stick) unsalted butter
150 grams (0.75 cups) castor (superfine) sugar
200 grams (7 ounces) ground blanched almonds
2 eggs
3 tablespoons brandy or rum (optional)
2 tablespoons apricot jam (jelly)
soaked dried apricots, poached peaches or plums
3 tablespoons flaked almonds for the topping

Method:
Line a 22-centimetre (8.5-inch) loose-bottomed flan tin with pastry and bake blind at 200°C (400°F) for 20 minutes until golden. To make the frangipane, cream the butter and sugar in a food processor. Add the ground blanched almonds, eggs and brandy (if desired) and blend well. Warm the jam, then spread over pastry case and spoon in frangipane mix. Cook at 180°C (350°F) for 15 minutes, then open oven and top tart with fruit, and scatter flaked almonds over the surface. Cook a further 10 minutes until tart is brown, almonds are golden and centre feels springy to the touch.
(Recipe reproduced with permission of Stephanie Alexander.)

9. Tropical Garden Style

The rousing popularity of the tropical style, lifestyle and architecture has gone hand in hand with the popularity of the frangipani—the signature flower of the tropics. The flower has become a well-known motif, and there are few who cannot recognise it. It forms the core of the tropical garden style, which started in the East, but has now been interpreted by numerous clever designers around the world.

The principle of tropical garden design is to find a balance between architecture and the landscape, blending them until you can't see where one finishes and the other begins. The relationship between nature, pools, fountains and foliage is sensory, tempting the visitor to look, feel and taste. These fusions have created a modern feel, which uses defined elements such as pavilions, pools, fountains, pergolas, water spouts and paving, alongside bold, luxurious plantings, contrasting textures, shapes, shadows and a play of light and shadow.

Tropical garden designers such as Brazil's Roberto Burle Marx, Bali's Made Wijaya (see Use in Design on page 130) and Hawai'i's Leland Miyano have revolutionised the way we view tropical gardens, while writers such as Lorraine Kuck and Richard Tongg have enriched gardeners' and horticulturists' knowledge with their books on tropical and subtropical flora.

The 'tropical garden movement' started with Roberto Burle Marx's (1909–94) swirling landscapes of rhythm, texture and imagination. 'I paint my gardens,' he liked to say. He liberated tropical gardens from the formality of European design. He unleashed a never-before-seen freedom into the garden, with patterns of bromeliad, heliconia, native grass and orchids. Plants were a dynamic force, as he put it:

OPPOSITE: Lightweight frangipani trunks frame this Balinese garden gateway. Batujimbar, Bali.

A garden is a complex of aesthetic and plastic intentions; and the plant is, to a landscape artist, not only a plant—rare and unusual, ordinary or doomed to disappearance—but it is also a colour, a shape, a volume or an arabesque in itself.

Robert Burle Marx

The father of modern tropical design, Sri Lanka's Geoffrey Bawa (1919–2003), helped us to see the building as part of the landscape, and the importance of integrating architecture with the environment. Bawa was the first to fuse elements of traditional Singhalese architecture with modern concepts of open planning. He developed this at his own home at Lunuganga, in Colombo's Bagatelle Road, and later with the artist Donald Friend in the development of the master plan for Batujimbar Pavilions, Bali (see Frangipanis in Art on page 193). This style of tropical architecture had a close relationship with nature, landscape and vegetation.

The tropical garden style is made up of abundant plantings of flowers and foliage, water, open pavilions, objects and ornament. This luxuriant 'jungle' atmosphere is naturalistic, and once you walk into it you feel relaxed and 'at one' with nature. To achieve this 'jungle' effect, the planting must be controlled or it can develop into chaos.

No landscape designer has done more to popularise the frangipani than Made Wijaya. His romantic tropical landscapes in Bali, Malaysia, Mauritius, Thailand, Singapore, India, Indonesia and the South Pacific have inspired generations of holidaymakers since the 1970s, ensuring the spread of frangipani fever throughout the world. Beginning with a breakthrough in 1981 at the Bali Hyatt hotel, he created a romantic blending of an English garden and tropical hedonism. His gardens transport you on a one-way ticket to paradise, where decadence, nuance, ornament, art and culture wash over you. He has designed hundreds of tropical gardens—domestic, public and hotel—around the world, including: Four Seasons Resort, Jimbaran, Bali; Taj Bentota Spa, Sri Lanka; Hyatt Aryaduta, Jakarta and Taj West End, Bangalore, India. For garden designers such as Wijaya, frangipanis satisfy many criteria: they are easy to grow, they come in either a pendulous or upright (candelabra) form, their trunks develop a silver patina with age, they can be trimmed within an inch of their lives and they transport well.

Get Your Hands Dirty

Gardening in the tropics and subtropics requires a different approach from cool-climate gardening. Maintaining tropical gardens is essential; they are not a set-and-forget solution. Early morning is the best time to garden, before the heat and humidity build up.

Anyone who gardens in a warm, high rainfall climate knows that during wet periods your plants explode out of the ground, smothering all their neighbours. To maintain your design you will need to prune such plants into submission. The wet season's rapid growth must be tamed.

Don't allow vigorous growth to impact on your garden's sweeping lines, vistas and views. Thin out the foliage, let the light in and reveal the sky. You will need a good pair of secateurs, pruners, clippers and a shredder, so prune as you walk and finish at the shredder. All shredded pruning material should be composted.

As many of the plants are surface rooting, avoid digging, which will damage the roots. Instead build up the soil layer by layer, with compost, shredded prunings, fallen leaves, garden clippings and mulch. Take your lead from nature, where the mulch layer is a natural part of the forest floor.

Weeds are best pulled out by hand, so as not to damage any surface roots. Use herbicides with care and discretion. Fertilise before the main growing season, with organic materials such as seaweed, well-rotted manures and fish waste.

Gardening in the tropics is good for the budget too. You can easily propagate many plants that thrive in this climate. Cuttings can be made from stems, roots and leaves. Frangipani, bromeliads and cordylines can easily be struck from stem cuttings or grown from seed. Cuttings should be taken from healthy plants and usually placed in a warm, humid environment to hasten root development and prevent them from drying out. Frangipani cuttings require different treatment (refer to Propagation on page 94)

Division can be used to propagate plants with offshoots, a multi-stem or clumping growth habit, or with underground storage structures, such as rhizomes or tubers. Division involves cutting large clumps into smaller sections, making sure that each clump has an enough stems, leaves, roots and buds to survive transplanting. Use this technique to propagate ferns, orchids, daylilies, bulbs, clivea, agapanthus and liriope.

Fellowship of the Frangipani

A garden designer is part sculptor, part engineer and part midwife, for his 'paint box' is filled with living things'.

Made Wijaya

As gardeners, we need to get to know the colours and textures in our paint box so we can paint better pictures. We believe that the fellowship of the frangipani is important too. In this chapter we explore some of the many plants that grow well with frangipani. No matter whether you live in the tropics, subtropics or temperate climates, you will find inspiration here to help your frangipani feel at home.

In Mexico and Panama, where frangipanis are native, they naturally grow in the wild with Vanilla, Moth and Crucifix Orchids. In the tropical dry forest habitats of Mexico, you can even find the frangipani growing side-by-side with cactus. This shows how resilient the frangipani is to long periods of dry weather, so if you live in a drier area, don't worry, your frangipani will be fine.

Even though the frangipani itself spans a range of climates, its companions rarely do. Your choice of companion plants will depend on where you live, considering limiting factors such as low winter temperatures, humidity and incidence of frost. It is helpful for home gardeners to have a good understanding of the climate in which they live before even beginning to design their garden. The following paragraphs give a rundown of the three main types of climate.

The tropics are the geographical area either side of the equator, between the Tropic of Cancer in the Northern Hemisphere and the Tropic of Capricorn in the Southern Hemisphere. This climatic zone usually has high precipitation for one part of the year and high humidity year round, and can be further divided into wet tropics and dry tropics. This applies to the frangipani growing regions of Costa Rica, Panama, Hawai'i, Thailand, Bali, Indonesia, Pacific islands, northern Australia and southern Florida. Tropical cities include Bangkok, Honolulu, Singapore, Denpasar and Darwin.

The subtropical climate is that found in the zone immediately north and south of the Tropic of Cancer and the Tropic of Capricorn. Loosely the range of latitudes is between 23.5 and 35 degrees north and south and includes warm and cool-temperate zones. The region generally exhibits warm temperatures and meagre precipitation. These areas have very warm to hot summers, but mild winters with air temperatures that do not go below freezing. The term applies to areas of coastal Australia, coastal South Africa, coastal California and southern Florida. Subtropical cities include New Delhi, Athens, Mexico City, Los Angeles and Brisbane. There may be microclimates within these cities that have colder than normal winter temperatures, which can make it difficult to establish healthy frangipanis and other subtropical plants.

The temperate latitudes of the globe lie between the subtropics and the polar circles, between around 35 degrees and 66.5 degrees latitude north and south. Frost is prevalent in the cool part of the zone, making frangipani growing possible only in a microclimate situation within the garden, where the plants are protected from frost and cold winds. Alternatively, frangipanis may be grown as heated glasshouse or conservatory subjects (see Overwintering on page 80).

If you design in the tropical garden style, with frangipani as the focus and with these climatic zones in mind, you will be well on your way to creating your own piece of paradise. However, a word of warning: don't succumb to what we call 'zonal denial syndrome', in which you choose plants you like and not plants you can actually grow. This syndrome will end in failure. Frosts will be too severe, plants will die over winter, money will be wasted and hopes will be dashed—on the whole, an unsatisfactory process. Instead choose plants that fit with your microclimate, and you and your garden will be happy.

Tropical Climate Companions

Palms, bamboo and banana are the backbone of the tropical garden and good selection is the key to success. Tropical palms such as the Fishtail Palm (*Caryota mitis*), Foxtail Palm (*Wodyetia bifurcata*) and Bottle Palm (*Hyophorbe lagenicaulis*) are pretty palms which will set an immediate tropical mood. Clumping palms can be used to screen unwanted views, while the Traveller's Palm (*Ravenala madagascariensis*), although not a true palm, has a balanced scale adjacent to a frangipani. Clumps of Buddha Belly Bamboo (*Bambusa ventricosa*) will draw the eye to its sensational bulbous and segmented stems.

Foliage plants make up interesting ground patterns and are best when grouped in patches. Look for varieties such as Peacock Plant (*Calathea makoyana*), Calathea, Ctenanthe (*Ctenanthe* 'Silver Star'), *Stromanthe sanguinea*, Prayer Plant (*Calathea* sp.) and crotons (*Codiaeum variegatum* 'America', 'Petra' 'Interruptum') have colourful and boldly shaped leaves, which contribute in a significant way to the lushness and volume of a tropical garden.

Tropical canopy trees are for those with large gardens only, as their branches spread to give glorious shade. They include: Poinciana (*Delonix regia*), Golden Showers (*Cassia fistula*), Golden Trumpet Tree (*Tabebuia* sp.), the African Tulip Tree (*Spathodea campanulata*), the Monkeypod (*Samanea saman*) and Breadfruit (*Artocarpus altilis*). Smaller trees such as *Mussaenda* provide a massive floral display that coincides with frangipani flowering in tropical zones. Don't forget tropical fruit, especially mango, lychee, avocado, feijoa and loquat.

Tropical flowers are some of the most desirable plants to grow, but unless you live in a truly tropical zone, leave them to the experts. Particularly amazing is the range of Lobster's Claw or Crab's Claw (*Heliconia* sp.), which have banana-like leaves and parrot-shaped flowers and are also pollinated by hummingbirds. The Desert Rose (*Adenium* sp.) is excellent in pots as it forms unusual bulbous trunks like bonsai.

Ornamental flowering gingers are usually mentioned together, as they are all tropical plants that produce flowers and foliage from stems called rhizomes that run in or on the ground. Most are grown for their flamboyant flowers, although foliage is also a feature. They include species of *Cucurma*, *Alpinia*, *Hedychium*, *Zingiber*, *Globba*, *Etlingera*, *Elettaria* and *Costus*. Magnificent in clumps and swathes, plants such as Ruby Ginger (*Curcuma rubescens*), Shell Ginger (*Alpinia zerumbet*), Red Ginger (*Hedychium greenei*) and Calathea Ginger (*Zingiber collinsii*) usually die down in winter only to reappear in warmer weather.

Of all the ground covers, the plum-coloured Moses-in-a-Cradle (*Rhoeo purpurea*) is immensely useful as carpet beneath frangipani. 'Stretch' is an elongated variety with a strong purple underside on the foliage. 'Strike Me Pink' has pinky purple stripes. Use them under frangipanis, with cordylines, in pots and with hibiscus where this colourful foliage will give a purple zing to the floor of the garden.

Designers in the tropics have fun with attaching all kinds of 'softeners' to frangipanis to break the line of stark branches and give the garden a

OPPOSITE: A riot of frangipani colour and foliage surround this well-designed pool with colourful frog tile mosaic, the private residence of Bill Bensley, Bangkok. Multicoloured frangipanis provide a floral ceiling to the pool and echo in the colours of the mosaic and other foliages used in the garden. Contrasting textures and leaf shapes make a striking statement, the foliage of Alocasia, cycads and cordylines are placed together to create a jungle atmosphere.

'lived-in' feel. This needs deliberation and planning. Tropical orchids were made for the stout branches of frangipani: moth orchids (*Phalaenopsis* sp.) have spectacular butterfly shaped petals; colourful Cattleya Orchids and *Brassia warscewiczii* are wonderful companions in high humidity and dappled shade of the frangipani; while the Crucifix Orchids (*Epidendrum ibaguense*) and Tillandsia enjoys a frost-free position in full sun alongside a frangipani.

Climbers tend to run wild and must be contained. Prune them into submission at least once a year and let them escape at your peril. Golden Trumpet Vine (*Allamanda cathartica*), Jade Vine (*Strongylodon macrobotys*) and the Blue Trumpet Vine (*Thunbergia grandiflora*) are exotic flowering climbers for a fence, arbour, pavilion or trellis, but it is best not to grow them on frangipani, due to their strangling and tenacious natures.

We cannot forget the watery wonders of aquatic plants such as the Sacred Lotus (*Nelumbo* sp.) and the night and day flowering water lilies (*Nymphaea* sp.), which are essential in tropical and subtropical ponds and water pots. Their colours complement frangipanis and usually flower at the same time.

TOP: A clashing combination of canopies—pink frangipanis intertwine with the red poinciana (*Delonix regia*).

CENTRE: The Desert Rose (*Adenium* sp.) comes from the same family as frangipani and flowers simultaneously in tropical climates.

BOTTOM: Grow a fern garden beneath frangipani for a verdant view. Red ginger (*Costus*) in background. Halekoa Hotel, Hawai'i.

Subtropical Climate Companions

A subtropical climate is one with luxuriant foliage, lush undergrowth, and spiked above with palm or tree fern fronds. Here form takes precedence over flowers. The term 'subtropical' is used here not in the strict geographic sense but in reference to climates where the summers are warm and winters are mild and frost free.

If the sight of frangipani's contorted winter stems disturbs you, maybe you need to think about a disguise. Try winter-flowering poinsettias and bromeliads to distract you from naked stems. Birds' nest ferns rest happily in the crooks of branches. Epiphytic orchids will grow on branches and flower when the tree is deciduous. Similarly a night-flowering climbing cactus can be trained up through the canopy. Their fragrant flowers coincide with those of the frangipani, appearing at night as the heat of summer builds.

If you are on the hunt for something graceful, look no further than the palms, bamboos and banana. The Lady Palm (*Rhapis excelsa*) is a well-behaved, long-lived and slow-growing palm, which makes a great privacy screen. The Golden Cane Palm (*Dypsis lutescens*), Bangalow Palm (*Archontophoenix cunninghamii*), Bismarck Palm (*Bismarckia nobilis*), Chinese Fan Palm (*Trachycarpus fortunei*) and the Dwarf Date Palm (*Phoenix roebelenii*) are also excellent palms for the subtropical and warm-temperate garden. Frame vistas and create texture with soft and feathery clumping bamboos. Eye-catching specimens of Abyssinian Banana (*Ensete ventricosa*) or Ornamental Banana (*Musa velutina*) will sit in well, in scale with your garden.

Flowering trees include the spreading Jacaranda (*Jacaranda mimosifolia*) and the medium-sized orchid tree (*Bauhinia* sp.). These trees are spectacular when viewed from second-storey windows.

A recent trend with contemporary subtropical gardens is to use foliage plants in sculptural ways. Frangipanis, cordylines, elephant ears, succulents, cycads and flax are brought together in dramatic combinations. Bold foliage adds vibrancy, texture, dimension and drama. Designers call them 'architectural' plants because they have a strong form, colour and shape; we call them 'accents'. Accent plants catch the eye, providing mini focal points throughout a garden, with vibrant colour, unusual form, tactile textures or interesting leaf shape. Mauritius Hemp (*Furcraea foetida*) and Giant Yucca (*Yucca elephantipes*) are tough and colourful.

Cordylines are evergreen shrubs and total winners for all-year lushness. They have been hybridised to exhibit brightly coloured leaves. Examples include 'Orangeaid', 'Paradise Pink', 'Pink Diamond', 'Blonde Ambition', 'Rubra', 'Nigra' and 'Aussie Gold'. They are tough and easy to grow from 200-millimetre (8-inch) cuttings, and handsome when planted in groups, lines or swathes. Preferring semi-shade, they grow well under a frangipani and palms.

Foliage plants provide volume to the garden beds. Choose easy to grow plants such as monstera, Giant Taro (*Alocasia macrorrhiza*), Tree Philodendron (*Philodendron bipinnatifidum*), Black Elephant's Ear (*Colocasia illustris*), colourful coleus (*Solenostemon scutellarioides*), Fijian Firebush (*Acalypha wilkesiana*) and Elephant's Ear (*Alocasia* x *amazonica*). Taller foliage accents like Giant Strelitzia (*Strelitzia nicolai*) and New Zealand Cabbage Palm (*Cordyline australis*) provide spiky explosions.

Succulents make good ground covers and are drought-hardy, perfect in areas where nothing else will grow. Don't think they need full burning sun to grow—they prefer morning or dappled sun. They thrive in pots, but can be grown under frangipanis in the company of cordyline, canna and Angel's Trumpet. They are very easy to propagate, providing a cost-effective approach to filling large areas of garden. Some training is required during their first year to help to toughen them during dry periods. Water carefully in the first year after planting, allowing them to dry out completely between watering. This will help them to grow a good strong root system and they will be self-sufficient after that.

Flowers are also essential in the subtropical garden and those with fragrance are hard to refuse. Showy flowers, nocturnal scent and recurrent flowering make the Angel's Trumpet (*Brugmansia* sp.) impossible to resist. In subtropical or warm temperate gardens, it is hardly without flower in the summer and autumn months. In cooler climates it, like the frangipani, will have to be brought into glasshouse conditions or pruned back hard during winter. Depending on the winter lows *Brugmansia* will bounce back in spring. Flowers come in shades of lemon, white, pink and apricot and older specimens will have 500 flowers in a flush. Its gentle evening fragrance is unsurpassed, particularly the apricot. The only black mark against it is that it has poisonous leaves and flowers.

Gingers that do well in a subtropical zone include the blue gingers which aren't true gingers (*Dichorisandra thysiflora* and *D. reginae*), Blue Marble Ginger

OPPOSITE: Vibrant colour brings the tropics to the subtropics. Here coloured cordylines combine brilliantly with bright impatiens—all thriving under the boughs of frangipanis.

(*Alpinia coerulea*), the tiny White Ginger or 'Graceful Ginger' (*Hedychium gracile*), the Hieroglyph, Painted Spiral, or Spiral Ginger (*Costus pictus*) and Red Tower Ginger (*Costus barbatus*), some of which have the bonus of edible flowers which are great in salads.

Use climbers to mellow vertical surfaces and cascade over and up through your frangipani, as well as over walls, fences, sheds and arbours. Their flimsy foliage quickly softens any hard edges and they also provide intense colour. Climbing cactus with exquisite water lily-like flowers love the company of frangipani, preferring to climb into the interior branches and flower at the same time, although during the night. These are generally called queen of the night cactus (*Epiphyllum oxypetalum* and *Selenicereus* sp.).

Some plants prefer to grow on frangipanis rather than under them. These are called epiphytic plants and they are happy with living up in the branches. Create hanging gardens in boughs and branches for a multilayered tropical paradise. Tie these plants on with twine or old stocking or rest them in the crooks of branches, and they will soon establish aerial roots and make the frangipani home. Bromeliads grow happily on tree trunks and branches. Birds' Nest Ferns (*Asplenium* sp.) love the dappled shade within the canopy of frangipani. They are content to grow on the main trunk and in the crooks of branches. Rock Orchids (*Dendrobium* sp.) love growing on branches and make happy housemates.

Other flowering climbers for subtropical gardens include the white fragrant Madagascar Jasmine (*Stephanotis floribunda*), Brazilian Jasmine (*Mandevilla* hybrids 'Alice du Pont', 'White Fantasy' and 'Beauty Queen'), Rangoon Creeper (*Quisqualis indica*), Orange Trumpet Vine (*Pyrostegia venusta*) and the Wonga Wonga Vine (*Pandorea pandorana*).

Temperate climate companions such as mass plantings of canna lily, dahlia, yellow candles (*Pachystachys lutea*) purple-leafed fountain grass and century plant flower simultaneously in summer. Government House, Sydney, Australia.

Temperate Climate Companions

The challenge with the temperate climate is to select cold-hardy plants that look tropical. These plants should be able to survive cold winters and not die down. Look to Roberto Burle Marx for inspiration and his gardens of bromeliads, agaves and cycads.

Striped foliage creates startling displays. The hardy flax from New Zealand suits a tropical look in temperate climates. *Phormium* 'Yellow Wave' is one of the best, with golden-yellow stripes to lighten up the garden. Canna lily provides broad, colourful leaves and hot-coloured flowers. In hot climates it needs shade. In cool climates it needs sun. Essential for good growth and showy foliage is water—they must have enough. Some varieties have spectacular striped foliage: 'Tropicana' has burgundy, bronze, gold and green stripes, while 'Tropicana Gold' has green and gold stripes. *Canna* x 'Australia' has deep burgundy black leaves. In cool zones, canna lily, like frangipani will need to be moved indoors over winter. In warm climates canna can be divided and hacked back to ground level in winter for an explosion of growth in spring.

Colourful ground covers for dappled shade include bromeliads (*Vriesia, Guzmania, Alcantarea imperialis* 'Rubra'), while other foliage contrasts for the shady areas include *Plectranthus argentatus, Carex buchanii* and Sweet Flag (*Acorus gramineus* 'Ogon').

Ground covers for sunny spots include succulents with bold outlines and distinct shape. Some are dramatic and fearsome, like the prickly agaves, while others, such as *Echeveria* sp., are friendlier. The new leaves of smooth *Agave attenuata* swirl gracefully as they unfurl themselves from the main growing sheath. The thorny-leafed agaves have exciting patterns. In some varieties, as each new leaf unravels from its tightly clasped growing sheath, it reveals sculptured lines and intriguing patterns imprinted onto the new leaves like a watermark. Jade (*Crassula ovata* 'Variegata') is a common but reliable plant paired with frangipani.

Hibiscus is not to be snubbed, as it is one of the best flowers to create a tropical look in cooler climates. September Lily (*Clivea miniata*) and Pagoda Plant (*Justicia aurea*) are good in shaded areas while Gardenia (*Gardenia* sp.) has perfumed white flowers in the sun. Brazilian Walking Iris (*Neomarica caerulea*) and Norfolk Island Iris (*Dietes robinsoniana*) have similar strap leaves, with unusual iris-shaped flowers. Flowering climbers such as Dwarf Bougainvillea and Chinese Star Jasmine (*Trachelospermum jasminoides*) are cold hardy and frangipani-friendly.

Coastal Companions

Frangipanis love the coast, but few others share the same resilience. Sea Box (*Alyxia buxifolia*) is one that does; it's a relative of the frangipani, which thrives on cliff edges in sandy soil and rock. Noted Australian garden designer Edna Walling called it her 'native box'. Coastal plants such as African daisies (*Gazania* and *Arctotis* sp.), Felt Plant (*Kalanchoe beharensis*), the iridescent Blue Chalksticks (*Senecio serpens*), Cushion Bush (*Leucophyta brownii*) and Coastal Rosemary are excellent low plantings, which thrive in these conditions. Taller shrubs include the never fail Rock Rose (*Cistus* x *purpureus*). Lavender (*Lavandula* x *allardii*) also performs well.

Also Known as Frangipani

Many in the botanical kingdom want to hitch a ride on the success of the frangipani name, and it's easy to understand why. They have been given the 'frangipani' title due to their similar features, whether it's their white flowers, sweet perfume, glossy leaves or frangipani-like flowers. The following three plants are not of the genus *Plumeria*, although some of them belong to the same family.

Frangipani Vine
Chonemorpha penangensis and *C. fragrans*

Family: Apocynaceae

Origin: Indo-Malaysia

Description: This is a magnificent climber, quite large and woody. Flowers are cream coloured, with a yellow centre. Summer bloomer. Flowers are beautiful, and dark green foliage is exquisite.

Similarity to frangipani: The flowers are more intensely fragrant than *C. fragrans*.

Size: 4 metres (13 feet)

Climate: Deciduous in subtropical climate and usually loses leaves if temperature drops below 15°C (59°F). Can survive mild frost for short periods.

Propagation: Cutting.

Use: Can be used as a fence cover or grown on a large trellis or pergola

Native Frangipani, Pong Pong or Sea Mango
Cerbera manghas and *C. odollam*

Family: Apocynaceae

Origin: Native to tropical Asia and Australasia, particularly Frangipani Beach in Cape York, Queensland.

Description: A small tree with dark foliage and showy, star-like white flowers borne from red-pink buds throughout the year. The calyx is green with pink overtones and is persistent on branch ends. The whorled leaves are crowded near the ends of thickish branches, with conspicuous leaf scars below. The flower petals overlap to the left and are hairy. The fruits are ellipsoid and speckled green drupes, often twinned.

Similarity to frangipani: Fragrant flowers are in the same arrangement as frangipani.

Size and habit: Small to medium-sized, 6 x 4 metres (20 x 13 feet).

Climate: Suited to tropical zones although semi-deciduous, often grown as an indoor plant in subtropical or temperate zones.

Use: Thrives in areas of strong and salt-laden winds, even shade.

Native Frangipani
Hymenosporum flavum

Family: Pittosporaceae

Origin: Queensland, Australia

Description: The native frangipani is one of the prettiest and most popular rainforest trees in Australia. It has a narrow, upright habit of growth. Yellow flowers turning orange with age occur in spring and early summer. They are followed by woody capsules, which contain winged seeds.

Similarity to frangipani: Sweet perfume, glossy leaves

Size and habit: Medium tree to 8 metres (26 feet), but may grow taller in gardens. Narrow growth habit makes it a good tree for small gardens.

Climate: Grows well in dry Mediterranean climates if additional water is available. Needs reasonably well-drained soil with a high organic content. Plants flower best in an open, sunny position but will grow successfully in shady places. Established plants will tolerate moderate frost.

Use: Feature tree, attracts birds, good for dappled shade and privacy.

10. Significance

In tropical regions, enthusiasts avidly search for frangipani collections and rarely are they disappointed. Botanic gardens around the world hold extensive collections. In Asia, frangipanis are signature trees around ancient temples and monuments, and frangipanis themselves are eagerly sought as offerings. Others will enjoy frangipanis in modern resort gardens in the tropics, where large hotels, resorts and spas use the trees to great effect.

Temples, Public Parks and Historic Homes

Throughout the East and the West, frangipanis are a prime choice for public-space plantings, due to their stature and splendour plus manageable size. In temples, public parks, historic homes, palaces and government buildings, they have a dignity and reverence that is respectful of their surrounds.

Soon after their arrival in the East, frangipanis were planted in temples. A good example is at Khantika Chatiya, in Sri Lanka, where they grow in the gardens of one of the oldest stupas (Buddhist monuments), which was built from 109–19 AD.

The French were early colonists in the West Indies. The French botanist Charles Plumier has been recognised, with his name given to the beloved frangipani genus. In Laos and Cambodia there are also strong French influences because of early colonisations. In these countries 'Celadine' is the favoured frangipani and has been adopted as the national flower of Laos. It is fondly known as 'White Champa'. (*Plumeria obtusa* is called 'Crying Champa' and is most commonly grown as a cemetery offering. This is the flower of sadness—perhaps because the flowers discolour disappointingly quickly after picking. To even walk under this tree is considered bad luck.)

Century-old frangipani trees surround the hilltop palace of Petchaburi, Khao Wang, Thailand.

In Laos, the UNESCO World Heritage site, Luang Prabang on the banks of the Mekong River, has an avenue of 100-year-old frangipanis leading up the steps to the top of Mount Phu Si, opposite the Royal Palace. And in Wat Phu, built between the tenth and thirteenth centuries, frangipanis line the wonderful Naga stairway.

In Buddhist culture 'Celadine' is revered for its colour. The yellow is symbolic of the robes of monks and white for goodness, friendship, peace and justice. Of the flower structure, the five petals equate with the five Buddhist precepts of the Moral Code: do not kill; do not steal; do not tell lies; do not indulge in adultery; and do not take intoxicants. Is it any wonder that 'Celadine' became a favourite and was planted widely from its first introduction to areas where the Buddhist faith had followers? As Buddhist offerings, the flowers are popular table decorations and from them scented water is made and given as a New Year's gift.

In Tahiti, if you visit the grave of the artist Paul Gauguin, at Calvaire Cemetery, on Hiva Oa Island, you will see that he's buried under a lone, old and gnarled frangipani. Frangipanis are commonplace on the islands of Tahiti and are used for decoration in the home and on the body. They are grown with Vanilla orchids, Tahiti's biggest export, which use the branches of the frangipani for support.

Some Eastern countries attach a very different meaning to the tree. In Malaysia locals know the frangipani as the Bunga Kubur or Graveyard Flower, and it is planted in graveyards to protect against evil spirits. Similarly, in Indonesia they are mainly used as a graveyard tree, Hindu Bali being the only exception.

Traditionally, in China and Thailand, frangipanis were considered unlucky in non-religious and non-royal compounds. They were mostly planted as boundary markers within Chinese cemeteries and therefore associated with the dead. It has taken many years to shrug off this reputation, and it has largely been as a result of skilful breeding, promotion and collection by enthusiasts. Frangipani interest in Thailand has grown over recent years, so much so that even their name has changed here. They are now promoted with the name Leelawadee (or Lilavadee or Lilawalee), which, according to some sources, was launched to replace the name Lan-tom, which is similar to the Thai word *ran-tom* which means 'heartbreak'.

Thailand's best frangipani collection is in Lilawalai Gardens, two hours from

Bangkok. This resort has 22 hectares (55 acres) of frangipani trees, numbering 1000 cultivars. The Lilawalai resort is surrounded by a grove of tropical flowering trees, and the water ponds are formed with the spring water from Khao Yai National Park. While frangipanis are rare in private gardens, they are often seen in religious and royal gardens; there are many at Petchaburi's hilltop palace, Khao Wang, which was built by King Rama IV in the mid-nineteenth century. Frangipanis over a century old are common here, planted in the gardens and around buildings.

ABOVE: Frangipanis are planted around every temple, Thailand.

We have already mentioned the relevance of the frangipani to the people of Bali, but it is important to note the use of the tree in traditional Hindu temples and water gardens here. A flawless tree sits beside Bale Kambang (the Floating Palace) in Klungkung, Bali. It has been given enough space to develop into the striking specimen it is today. The open-air Bale Kambang is one of Klungkung's most important structures, built in the sacred area of the compound. An artificial pond, once covered in water lilies, surrounds the pavilion. When I visited it was planted with potted Desert Rose (*Adenium* sp.) in flower.

Not far away, in the town of Ubud, Pura Taman Saraswati (The Lotus

BELOW: Immaculately trimmed frangipani tree, at the Floating Palace, Klungkung, Bali.

Temple), built in 1898, features water gardens filled to the brim with lotus, in full flower, fruit and bud. Twin frangipanis flank the temple's entrance, open every day. This peaceful retreat is focused on flowers and fragrances that calm and refresh the spirit. Excellent examples of the 'Singapore' frangipani (*Plumeria obtusa*) can also be seen surrounding the water terraces of the recently restored Taman Ujung (Water Palace), on Bali's little-known east coast.

ABOVE: Frangipanis frame the entrance to the Lotus Temple at Pura Taman Saraswati, Ubud, Bali.

LEFT: Ancient trees surround the ancient ruins of Emperor Tu Duc's Palace, Vietnam.

Sydney's Government House

In Australia, public parks designed in the Victorian era were adorned with bold groupings of plants. Sydney's Government House, on the foreshore of the harbour, has a magnificent view of the city, and the garden includes exotics such as cannas, ginger, phoenix palms, agapanthus, agave, yucca, flax and frangipani, which were used in a bold style that is back in vogue in Australia. The shape and proportion of these grandiose gardens was important, as the garden had to contend with larger trees, such as Bunya Bunya pines and Morton Bay figs, which tended to dominate the landscape and the skyline. Here frangipanis acted as the 'middle man'.

Sited on Bennelong Point, Government House was built between 1837 and 1845 in the Gothic Revival style. The building was seen to reflect the colony's maturity as it reached the end of convict transportation and moved towards responsible government. As such, the house sits within an important historic garden with exotic trees, long lawns, shrubs, carriageways, formal paths and terraces. Two feature frangipani trees, approximately 80 years old, are in good condition and have inspired further plantings along the garden terraces.

This frangipani tree, approximately 80 years old, has inspired further plantings along the garden terraces of Government House, Sydney, Australia.

Dean Conklin Plumeria
Grove, Koko Crater,
Oahu, Hawai'i,

Botanic Gardens and Collections

Modern-day collections have sprung up in the tropical world celebrating the
popularity of this flower. Dean Conklin Plumeria Grove, located in the outer
crater of Koko Crater, Oahu, Hawai'i, is another must for the frangi-fanatic.
The garden contains about 60 named and unnamed varieties, which are mature,
towering up to 10 metres (33 feet) high, and can be easily viewed from an
oval pathway inside the crater. The end of April is the best time of year to visit
the collection, as most trees are in full flower. The majority are labelled, with
accession numbers for others. Here frangipani seeds germinate readily wherever
they fall, so tread lightly under the trees (see also Hawai'i on page 34).

Other gardens in Hawai'i, such as the Limahuli Botanical Garden, Kauai, and the Kahanu Garden, Maui, have small collections of frangipani in incredibly scenic locations. Not far from Poipu, Kauai, on the cliffs of the Lawa'i Valley are the Allerton Gardens, once the retreat of Hawai'i's Queen Emma. A frangipani grove has recently been planted in an area adjacent to the gardens, including a number of named cultivars such as 'Rainbow', 'Katie Moragne', 'Ruffles', 'Mela Matson', 'Carter Selection', 'Tomlinson Pink', 'Loretta', 'Elena', 'Samoan Fluff', 'Gardenia' and 'Kimi Moragne'.

However, the undisputed paradise for plumeria lovers is in Thailand. Nong Nooch Tropical Botanical Garden, Chonburi, has a world-class collection of tropical plants, including cycads, palms and climbers, as well as one of Asia's largest private collections of frangipanis. The garden was begun in 1954, when Mr Pisit and Mrs Nongnooch Tansacha bought land on the Sukhumvit Road in the Chonburi province. Mrs Tansacha decided to turn the existing fruit orchard into a tropical garden of ornamental flowers and plants. Nong Nooch Tropical Botanical Garden has an extensive collection of 500 frangipani varieties outside its 'palmetum', many of which were collected from around the world. An avenue of mature specimens can be seen in full bloom outside the Nantha Seminar Building.

Frangipanis are collected in the West too. Australia's Brisbane Botanic Gardens—at Mt Coot-tha a good collection of approximately 100 frangipanis, which include six species and a number of named and unnamed cultivars from the Department of Primary Industries, Bowen Research Station. The variety 'Fruit Salad' (syn. 'Apricot Delight' and 'Apricot') is of particular interest, as it's an Australian-grown series, which is hugely popular throughout the country. This subtropical botanic garden is 15 minutes from the city, with frangipanis spread throughout the garden.

Miami's Fairchild Tropical Botanic Garden, built in 1938 is a 34 hectare (83-acre) garden, which encompasses the plants from the original private collection of Colonel Robert Montgomery. Plumeria species include *Plumeria alba, P. cubensis, P. obtusa, P. obtusa* var. *obtusa, P. obtusa* var. *sericifolia, P. pudica, P. rubra* and *P. jamaicensis*. Cultivars include 'Bali Whirl', 'Daisy Wilcox', 'Heidi', 'Japanese Lantern', 'Kauka Wilder', 'Key West Red', 'Koko Monster', 'Lei Rainbow', 'Madame Poni' and eight other accessions.

South Texas Botanical Gardens and Nature Center, once known as the

Corpus Christi Botanic Gardens, has a collection of 92 plumerias. There are 56 different cultivars now located in two areas, and the garden's authorities have recently moved the plants to a new and more visible area, which includes sidewalks and a viewing ramp in the centre of the garden. At the time of writing, they had been unable to put all of the plants in one place until more work was done at the site.

The Matrimandir Gardens in Auroville, India, are a botanical paradise with a number of sections. Frangipani have been selected to represent the Garden of Perfection. The garden has had a long association with Richard and Mary Helen Eggenberger.

ABOVE: Mt Coot-tha Botanic Garden in Brisbane, Australia, has an excellent collection of frangipanis.

OPPOSITE TOP: Matrimandir Gardens, Auroville, India.

OPPOSITE BELOW: Potted frangipani bananas, bromeliads, ferns and palms are on display in the glasshouse. Nong Nooch Tropical Botanical Gardens, Thailand.

11. Decoration and Art

Travelling through the tropics you quickly notice the intense colour, fragrance and variety of frangipanis. They decorate hotels, lobbies and gardens, in float bowls, urns, vases, ponds, pools, leis, on beds and scattered along pathways. They are the essence of the tropics. In Bali they combine with Globe Amaranth, *Allamanda*, hibiscus, bougainvillea and tuberose in woven baskets that are placed on altars, in cars, on pavements and even strung over motorbike handles to give good fortune. In the West the fragrance has become popular in weddings, beauty treatments and creams and as a symbol of a tropical lifestyle; the frangipani blossom motif, either naturalistic or stylised, has been widely adopted, to the point, for some people, of hovering on the border between acceptability and kitsch. Postcards, posters, car windows, ornaments, jewellery, china, fabrics ... there seems no limit to the consumer items adorned with frangipanis.

Artists in tropical regions have long been captivated by the simplicity and beauty of the frangipani blossom. Artists such as Paul Gauguin and Donald Friend depicted the trees and flowers as a part of tropical island life.

Some 1940s postcards from Hawai'i featuring frangipani.

Decorating with Frangipani

The use of the frangipani motif as a decorative symbol is far from a recent phenomenon. When the Mayan civilisation reached its peak, from 300–900 AD, images of flowers were significant to this agricultural society. On clothing they denoted rank, while on buildings they had perhaps the same meaning, appearing in friezes and cornice mouldings. A five-petalled disc motif which was used repeatedly may well be a stylised frangipani. After the Mayan culture was destroyed by Spanish colonisation, architecture displayed a blending of traditional Spanish elements with floral motifs as decoration.

The Lei

Lei is the Hawaiian term for garland or wreath. The fresh flower necklace is used as a traditional Hawaiian greeting, and can symbolise friendship, love, reverence, respect, congratulations and welcome. These days they are presented in their thousands at airports and passenger terminals throughout the Pacific, but originally they were used in a variety of ways—as decoration, in the hula, in ceremonies and in peace agreements between chiefs.

There are many different types of leis and many reasons to give one. The wreaths or garlands can be made of shells, feathers, bone, seeds and flowers— an exceptional floral lei can be composed of up to 800 individual flowers.

There are two different methods used to join the flowers: threading with a needle through the centre of the flower or tying flowers individually by the stem. Sometimes three separate strings of flowers may be braided together.

The easiest method is the first and requires 50–70 fresh flowers, a length of fishing line or strong thread and a lei needle, which has a hook at one end. Gather the flowers early in the morning, and for best results use flowers that have a thick, waxy feel, such as 'Celadine', 'Nebel's Rainbow' and 'Hilo Beauty'. These flowers have a two to three day keeping quality once they are made into a lei.

Work out what pattern you desire and start to string the flowers onto the needle, from front to back, sliding them two or three at a time down the string—no more otherwise they will tear.

Dip the needle into Vaseline to make it slide through more easily. Once you've finishing stringing the flowers, cut the string and tie the ends. Wear straight away or keep it in a plastic bag filled with air and a splash of water until you need it. Refrigeration helps them to last and a light spray with water will refresh them.

You can also revive the lei by totally immersing it into water overnight; the flowers will plump up ready for another day.

E lei aku 'oe ku'u aloha I ko'olua nou
  I kahi mehameha.

Wear my love as a lei, and as your companion in lonely places.

Traditional Hawaiian Song

One of the most popular leis is the *melia lei*. It is made from frangipani flowers which keep their fragrance for several days, even after drying. In Hawai'i, plumeria are judged solely on how good their flowers are for lei-making. 'Celadine' flowers are by far the preferred choice because of their 'substance', and therefore keeping quality, and good perfume, which is important to the buying public. It is interesting to note that *Plumeria obtusa* is quite unsuitable for leis, as it browns quickly. Lei shops in Honolulu's Chinatown sell the best leis in the world, and you can visit Sunset Beach on Oahu's north shore to see plantations for the lei-making industry.

Hawaiian Lei Day, 1 May, is a holiday on which everyone wears leis, and there is a lei-making contest in schools. Another festival day is 11 June, Kamehameha Day, which celebrates the first ruler to unite the islands two centuries ago. King-sized strands of glossy leaves twined with yellow frangipanis—symbolising the feather cloaks traditionally worn by royalty—trail 14 metres

TOP: Author Linda Ross adorned in frangipanis, Tweed Heads, Australia.

BELOW: This simple lei was made for us by Kim Packman from DJ's Nursery in Tweed Heads. Made from 80 flowers they were strung onto a lei needle and lasted beautifully.

(45 feet) from the large statue of King Kamehameha at Waikiki Beach, Honolulu.

Floral Art

Frangipani flowers last well in float bowls but are rarely used in vases, as they can be difficult to arrange, with their thick branches and bleeding stems. Being white and fragrant, frangipani is popular for bridal bouquets along with stephanotis, jasmine and gardenia. The wedding bouquet can be constructed in many shapes—sphere, teardrop or trailing, in which case each flower is individually wired. Frangipani hairpin decorations are popular for wedding guests, and frangipani flowers are often used to carpet the floor around the church and reception.

When arranging frangipanis yourself, start by wiring flowers individually or attaching them onto toothpicks for small vases or simpler arrangements. Frangipanis can last like this for up to five days. The toothpick method is also a good idea for hair decorations.

To individually wire flowers for bouquets, use small gauge wire (22 gauge) and push the wire into the calyx—the base of the frangipani head, the hardest part—and bend it back. Wrap with parafilm (available at florists) to secure wire to flower. Once the flower has been wired, twirl the stem while stretching and pulling the green parafilm tape (available from florists) around the wire at a downward angle. The tape should be tightly wrapped around the wire and flower stem without buckles or gaps along the stem. Fasten off just above the end of the wires by squeezing the parafilm tape against itself. Do this to as many flowers as you need.

Then arrange the individual flowers into a sphere, teardrop or oval-shaped bouquet with a little greenery. Tie the bouquet with string or a green ribbon to hold it in place. Using a wide satin ribbon, bind the stems tightly to form a hand-hold. Secure the ribbon by pushing pearl-head pins into the ribbon and towards the centre of the bouquet stems, ensuring the sharp ends of the pins are hidden.

ABOVE: Two dances in Bali, the *rejang* and the *legong*, require dancers to wear ornate frangipani headdresses. Hindu and Indian influences are significant in Balinese dancing, as are various influences from indigenous animist religions and folklore traditions, creating a unique expression of Balinese ethnicity.

OPPOSITE: *Plumeria obtusa* flowers are individually pinned through a toothpick to stand up straight in this miniature bouquet.

TOP: A simple green glass bowl with floating frangipani flowers will last up to five days before they lose their fragrance.

BELOW: Vase with quick arrangement that will last for days.

OPPOSITE TOP LEFT: Frangipani flower carpet at author's wedding. Tirtha Uluwatu, Bali.

OPPOSITE TOP RIGHT: White frangipani bouquet at author's wedding. Tirtha Uluwatu, Bali.

OPPOSITE BELOW LEFT: Mixed pink bouquet for bridesmaids at author's wedding.

OPPOSITE BELOW RIGHT: A thick carpet of flowers decorates the aisle of this chapel. Cut flowers are becoming a large market worldwide.

Tab. XI.

PLUMERIA *flore roseo odoratissimo* *Jus.R.H.*

Published by G. D. Ehret. Nov. 1799.

Frangipanis in Art

Countless artists have succumbed to the allure of frangipanis—Donald Friend, Paul Gauguin and Brett Whiteley are among them.

In 1705 the Swiss naturalist and artist Maria Sibylla Merian (1647–1717) sailed to the Dutch colony of Suriname (Dutch Guiana) in South America. A series of copper etchings of flowers and insects was produced from her sketches. Her *Metamorphosis Insectorum Surinamensium* included the Red Jasmine Tree, *Plumeria rubra*. First published in Amsterdam in 1705, this collection was supplemented with posthumous publications in 1726 and 1730.

Mark Catesby (1683–1749) a botanist, travelled from England to America in 1712, sketching plants and animals, and sending collections of plants and seeds back to England over a period of seven years. He made a return trip in 1722, and his collection of botanical sketches resulted in a monumental work, *The Natural History of Carolina, Florida and the Bahama Islands*—the most famous colourplate book on American natural history before Audubon's *Birds of America*. Among the collection was plate 92, from Volume II: 'Plumeria Flore Roseo Odoratissimo', the Red Frangipani.

Frangipani and Hummingbird is a striking painting by Brett Whiteley, one of Australia's most significant twentieth-century artists, who is represented in

OPPOSITE: One of the first botanical sketches of frangipani ever drawn. Completed by Mark Catesby (1683–1749).

BELOW: *Frangipani and Hummingbird*. 1988. Oil and tempera on canvas. 211 x 400 cm. Painting by Brett Whiteley.

all major Australian collections. Selling in 2006 for A$2.04 million, it was an all-time record for an Australian artist. Described as a monumental canvas, not least for its size, it is an evocative work revealing Whiteley's love of birds and frangipanis. It was painted in a period of frenetic creativity before his death. The Sotheby's description of the painting at the time of auction was itself an evocation of the passion in the work:

> *In* Frangipani and Hummingbird *the delicacy of flower and feathered creature, small in reality but seen here as though in a most intimate close-up view, contrasts with the dramatic scale and palette of the work. Whiteley had previously painted a number of views of Sydney Harbour that included frangipani trees, with their distinctive silhouette and heavily scented white and gold blossoms. However, here it is almost as though in viewing the painting we zoom in alongside the tiny bird seeking nectar from a single bloom. Tropical warmth, the sweet perfume of frangipani, even the suggestion of sound—the humming of tiny wings—are all evoked with great subtlety, whilst, in masterly counterpoise, the sense of movement is kaleidoscopic and the colour is almost explosive in its brilliance.*

Whiteley's former wife, Wendy Whiteley, said that, 'He identified with birds and has painted them over and over again. Certain trees and birds are symbolic of his work'.

The Indonesian artist Dullah's portrait of a Balinese girl, *Miss Sasih*, dressed in traditional costume and picking up a fallen white bloom, shows the relevance the frangipani flower has to the Balinese culture. Here the frangipani is an important flower of the Hindu faith (92 per cent of Balinese are Hindu). Frangipani trees are often planted in the family compound to provide flowers for daily offerings and as decoration for the traditional legong dancer's headdress. The trees often flank shrines in the courtyard of the home. There are more than 20,000 temples in Bali, and ceremony and tradition in village life is essential. As Made Wijaya says, 'If you are Balinese, you go to the temple and take part in all village activities. Or you leave'.

The first time I saw a frangipani, I was in Tahiti. I was aware of a soft and sensual perfume in the breeze. It was a scent that I could not identify. The next time that I was conscious of that fragrance, I was threading lush, white flowers to create a lei. The frangipani is easy to thread. At this time of year when the first flakes of snow arrive, I think of Bora Bora and the frangipani, which grows there in abundance. I can almost smell them as I paint them.

Canadian artist, Barbara Simmons

OPPOSITE LEFT: *Miss Sasih (Ni Sasih)*. 1977. Oil on canvas, 100 x 70 cm. Painting by Dullah.
ABOVE: *Frangipani*. 56 x 38 cm. Painting by Barbara Simmons.

Appendix:

Specimens, Nurseries and Gardens

Frangipanis are found the world over and are fast becoming one of the world's most desirable collectable plants. Here is where you'll find the best-named collections and specimens worldwide.

Thailand

Nong Nooch Tropical Botanical Gardens, Chonburi
Anantara Resort and Spa, Huan Hin
Evason Resort and Spa, Huan Hin
Bill Bensley residence, Bangkok
Lilawalai Gardens, near the Khao Yai National Park, Bangkok
Petchaburi's Mountain Palace 'Khao Wang', near Hua Hin
Royal Garden Village, Hua Hin
Wat Raj Bophit, Bangkok
The Regent, Mae Rim District, 30 kilometres from Chiang Mai
Jack's Nursery, near Chiang Mai
Danney's Nursery, near Chiang Mai
Nok's Nursery, Bangkok
Widget Plumeria Resort, Pattaya Beach
Chatachuk Markets (mid week), Bangkok

LEFT: An unidentified Moragne seedling, Hawai'i.

Vietnam

Tomb of Emperor Tu Duc, Hue

Laos

The ruin of Wat Phou, Champassak

The Royal Palace, Luang Prabang Palace

Vat Phou Champasak World Heritage Site

Malaysia

The Mines Resort, Kuala Lumpar

Singapore

Singapore Botanic Garden

The Farm, San Benito

Adam Park Resort

Andrew Road Villas

Wee Ee Chong House

Bali

Begawan Giri, Ubud

Batujimbar, Sanur

The Ritz Carlton, Bali Resort and Spa, Jimbaran Bay

Villa Umah di Beji, Canggu

Tirtha Uluwata, Uluwata

Tirtha Gangga, Karangasem

Taman Ujung (The Floating Palace)

Villa Ylang Ylang, Sanur

Jimbaran Peninsula

Puri Ganesha, Pemuteran

Puri Taman Saraswati (Lotus Temple), Ubud

The Bali Hyatt, Sanur

Nusa Dua Beach Hotel, Nusa Dua

Puri Santrian, Sanur

Griya Santrian Hotel, Sanur

Westin Hotels and Resort, Nusa Dua

Villa Kirana, Sayan, Ubud

Four Seasons Resort, Jimbaran

Australia

Mt Coot-tha Botanic Gardens, Brisbane, Queensland

Government House, Sydney, NSW

Royal Botanic Gardens, Sydney, NSW

DJ's Nursery, Tweed Heads, Queensland

Bronte House, Bronte, Sydney, NSW

Roma Street Gardens, Brisbane, Queensland

Sacred Gardens Frangipani Nursery, Mount Garnet, Queensland

Tahiti

Paul Gauguin Museum, Tahiti
Paul Gauguin Grave, Calvary Cemetery, Hiva 'Oa, Marquesas Islands

USA

The Mauna Kea Beach Hotel, Honolul, Oahu, Hawai'i
Grove Farm, Kauai, Hawai'i
Fairchild Botanic Gardens, Florida
Dean Conklin Grove at Koko Crater Botanic Gardens, Oahu, Hawai'i
South Texas (formerly Corpus Christi) Botanical Gardens & Nature Centre
Limahuli Garden, Kaua'i, Hawai'i
Allerton Garden, Kaua'i, Hawai'i
Po'ipu Island, Kaua'i, Hawai'i
Foster Botanic Gardens, Honolulu, Oahu, Hawai'i
Florida Colors Nursery, Florida
Teas Nursery, Texas
Stokes Tropicals, Louisiana
Smokey Acres Lei Farm, Oahu, Hawai'i
Jim Little Nursery (mail order), Hawai'i.

China

Xishuangbanna Botanic Tropical Gardens, Yunnan Province

Sri Lanka

Bentota Beach Hotel, Bentota

India

Matramundir Gardens, Auroville, Tamil Nadu

Glossary

accessions	plants added to horticultural collections.
aeration	the improvement of drainage by increasing the size and number of air pockets in the soil.
air layering	a reliable form of propagation commonly used on varieties deemed hard to strike from cuttings.
alternate	a common leaf arrangement with leaves on opposite sides of stems at successive nodes.
anthers	the ends of stamens, bearing the pollen.
anti-transpirant	a fine film of liquid applied to reduce moisture loss.
apex	the topmost growing tip of the plant.
apical grafting	the process whereby the scion is attached to the apex of the plant.
backfill	the material replaced after soil is removed.
balanced appearance	the natural symmetrical shape that a tree achieves without any pruning.
bare-rooted	the plant condition when it is lifted from the ground, and soil is lost from the roots.
branch tips	the ends of branches.
calyx	the outer whorl of sepals enclosing the corolla.
cambium	the layer of rapidly dividing cells found between the bark and the wood—of special importance in grafting.
centres	the spacing selected for planting multiple trees.
convolute	rolled up lengthwise with overlapping edges.
corolla	the whorl of petals together.
cotyledons	the seed leaves paired in germinating seedlings.

OPPOSITE: 'Kirra Dawn'.

cultivars	named cultivated varieties selected for their characteristics and which are retained from one generation to the next.
culture	successful cultivation and care (usually outdoors).
damping off	collapse of young seedlings due to fungal attack.
deciduous	leaves falling off, usually as a reaction to shortening, cooler autumn days.
dehiscence	natural splitting of fruit to release seeds.
drip line	the region at ground level, below the tree at the extremity of foliage.
elliptical	oval shaped.
epiphytic	growing on a host plant but not parasitic on it.
friability	the loose and crumbly nature of soil, desirable for plant growth.
fruit set	the extent of the fruit crop as a response to pollination.
genus	a group of closely related species.
germ plasm	material collected that contains the genetic code to reproduce the entire plant.
girdling	a procedure undertaken to facilitate the strike rate of cuttings.
grafting	the propagation process of uniting a part of the desired variety (scion) with the stem or roots of another (understock).
habit	the appearance and style of growth, especially the way the main branches are held.
heartwood	the inner part of the stem.
hue	colour, including tones, tints and shades.
hybrid	a plant resulting from the crossing of two different species.
imbrication	overlapping of petals.
indented	with an irregular or wavy leaf margin.
inflorescence	cluster of flowers.
laticifer	an elongated secretory cell producing latex.
lanceolate	a long, oval-shaped leaf with pointed tip.

laterals	smaller branches coming from the main structural branches.
latex	sticky sap; milky white in frangipanis.
loam	the most desirable soil type, being a good balance of sand and clay.
lobe	a protruding part of a leaf or petal.
lopping	heavy pruning.
margins	the edges; usually of leaves.
mulch	material spread over the soil surface to retain moisture and suppress weeds.
node	the point on a stem from hich leaves emerge.
nomenclature	system of naming plants. A two-word (binomial) system of genus followed by species is the usual botanical name recognised throughout the world.
obovate	oval shaped but with a broader end near the apex or distal end of leaf or petal.
passive solar home	a design technique that uses position and aspect to control microclimate without the use of additional energy in the form of air conditioning and heating.
pedicel	the stalk of a single flower.
peduncle	the main stalk of an inflorescence.
pendulous	slightly weeping appearance of branches, leaves or inflorescences.
persistent	not deciduous, but remaining attached for an extended period.
petiole	the stalk of a leaf connecting the blade to the branch.
pistil	the female or seed bearing part of a flower, consisting of ovary, style and stigma.
potting on	the practice of replanting into a larger size container when the tree roots start to be restricted.
proboscis	an insect's sucking tube.
pubescent	covered with soft hairs.
raised beds	planting beds constructed of free-draining material on top of otherwise heavy soil.

recurved	folded over, usually referring to the leaf margins.
reflexed	folded back to varying degrees, usually referring to petals.
scion	a piece of the desired variety for grafting onto a sturdy understock.
seedling	a young plantlet resulting from the germination of a seed. The mature plant carries genetic characteristics of its two parents and therefore is not identical to the tree that produced the seed.
self-pollination	the process whereby pollen is transferred to the stigma of the same flower or another flower on the same tree.
semi-deciduous	shedding only a proportion of leaves each season.
spatulate	spatula-shaped, with a narrow base and wider end.
species	a group of plants essentially alike because of similar genetic make-up.
spent	refers to an inflorescence in which most flowers have fallen.
spiral	a whorled arrangement of leaves or petals.
stamen	the male part of a flower comprising a long filament and the pollen-bearing anther.
stigma	the upper, receptive part of a pistil, being the receptive surface for pollen.
style	the elongated part of the pistil connecting the ovary and stigma.
substance	the thickness and texture of petals that determines the flower's keeping quality after picking.
syn.	synonym.
systemic	insecticide that is taken up into the tissue of the plant, not the surface.
taxonomy	classification (grouping and arrangement) of plants, based on their botanical characteristics.
terminal	found at the ends of branches.

tissue culture	a laboratory technique of propagation under sterile conditions with the capacity to produce a large number of plants from a small amount of plant tissue.
top dress	an application to the soil surface of either fertiliser or further growing medium.
true to type	can be propagated from seed reliably to achieve plants identical to parents.
tubulate	tube-shaped.
umbellate cyme	an inflorescence in which the pedicels are of similar length; the central flowers open first.
understock	that part which forms the root system of a grafted tree.
understorey	vegetation that grows beneath the canopy of taller species.
UV	ultraviolet light.
variety	a distinctive form.
var.	abbreviation for variety.
volatile	readily vaporised.
washing soda	sodium carbonate, available in supermarket.
weeping	of pendulous habit.
white oil	'White Oil' or horticultural oil, either plant or petroleum based, is on the market for scale treatment.
whorled	with rings of three or more parts (usually leaves) around the stem.

References and Further Reading

Books

Aitken, R. (2006), *Botanical Riches*, Melbourne University Press, Melbourne.

Aitken, R. and Looker, M., eds (2002), *The Oxford Companion to Australian Gardens*, Oxford University Press in association with Australian Garden History Society, Melbourne.

Alexander, S. (1996), *The Cook's Companion*, Viking Penguin, Melbourne.

Bligh, B. (1973), *Cherish the Earth—the Story of Gardening in Australia*, Ure Smith, Sydney.

Brandies, M.M. (2004), *Landscaping with Tropical Plants,* Sunset Books, California.

Bremness, L. (1994), *Herbs*, Dorling Kindersley Publishing Inc, London.

Bunch, A.W. (2006), 'The Exotic Plumeria—a pictorial', vol.1, *The Flower of Hawaii*, The Exotic Plumeria Tropical Gardens Publishing.

Eggenberger, R. and M. (2000), *Handbook on Plumeria Culture*, Tropical Plant Specialists, Georgia, USA.

Eliovson, S. (1991), *The Gardens of Roberto Burle Marx*, Saga Press Inc, Singapore.

Garnett, T.R. (1996). *A Gardener's Guide to the Climatic Zones of Australia*, The Australian Garden History Society, Melbourne.

Grieve, M. (1931), *A Modern Herbal*, Penguin, Harmondsworth.

Hortus Third (1976), Macmillan Publishing Company, New York, USA.

Houston, S.D, ed. (1998), *Function and Meaning in Classic Maya Architecture*, Dumbarton Oaks Research Library and Collection, Washington DC.

Kingsbury, N. (1996), *Dramatic Effects with Architectural plants*, Mitchell Beasley, London.

OPPOSITE: 'Aussie Pink' smells like coconut. Sydney, Australia.

Lansing, J. Stephen, *Balinese Religion* in *The Encyclopaedia of Religion*, ed. Mircea Eliade, Macmillan, New York.

Little, J. (2006), *Growing Plumerias in Hawaii*, Mutual Publishing.

McDonald, M. (1978), *Ka Lei: The Leis of Hawaii,* Topgallant Publishing Co. Ltd, Honolulu, Hawaii.

McMaugh, J. (2000), *What Garden Pest or Disease is That?,* Lansdowne.

Macoboy, S. (1974), *Tropical Flowers and Plants*, Paul Hamlyn, Sydney.

Oakes, J. (1996), *The Book of Perfumes*, Harper Collins, Sydney.

Pellowski, A. (1990), *Hidden Stories in Plants*, Macmillan & Co., New York.

Stringer, L.A. and McAvoy L.H. (1995), 'The need for something different: Spirituality and Wilderness', in *The Theory of Experiential Education* (eds Warren K., Sakofs, M. and Hunt, J.S.), Kendall Hunt, Dubuque, Iowa.

Tettoni, L.I. and Warren, W. (1996), *Thai Garden Style*, Periplus Editions (K), Hong Kong.

Valder, P. (1999), *The Garden Plants of China*, Florilegium, Sydney.

Walker, J. (1996), *The Sub Tropical Garden,* Timber Press, Portland, Oregon.

Walling, E. (1943), *Gardens in Australia: Their Design and Care*, Oxford University Press, Melbourne.

Warren, W. (1991), *The Tropical Garden,* Thames and Hudson Ltd, London.

Warren, W. (2001), *Tropical Garden Plants,* Thames and Hudson Ltd, London.

Wijaya, M. (2000), *At Home in Bali*, Abbeville Press, New York.

Wijaya, M. (1999), *Tropical Garden Design*, Archipelago Press, Singapore.

Zabihi, K. and Jotisalikorn, C. (2005), *Contemporary Asian Pools and Gardens*, Periplus, Hong Kong.

Articles

Baston, E.S. (1895), 'Botanical Medical Monographs and Sundry, The Apocynaceae in Materia Medica', *American Journal of Pharmacy*, vol. 67, No. 3., p 18.

Burle Marx, R. (July 1988), 'A Garden Style in Brazil to Meet Contemporary Needs with Emphasis on the Paramount Value of Native Plants', in *Landscape Architecture* 44.

Burle Marx, W. (28–30 June 1954), Paper presented at the 55th Annual Meeting of the American Society of Landscape Architects, held in Boston.

Criley, R. and Little, J. (1991), 'The Moragne Plumerias', *American Horticultural Society*.

Criley, R.A. (Aug 1994), 'What is the True Plumeria Fragrance?', *Horticulture Digest*, issue 102, Department of Horticulture, University of Hawaii.

Criley, R.A. (Jan 2005), 'Plumeria in Hawaii', *Ornamentals and Flowers*, OF-31 College of Tropical Agriculture and Human Resources, University of Hawaii.

Haber, W.A. (1984), *Pollination by Deceit in a Mass-Flowering Tree—Plumeria rubra*, Biotropica, Vol. 16.

Schofield, L. (2004), 'A Flurry of Frangipanis in Frangipani Facts', issue 9, *Journal of the Frangipani Society of Australia*.

Sotheby's Catalogue, 'Catalogue notes', 2006.

Ulrich, R.S. (1984), 'View through a window may influence recovery from surgery', *Science*, 224. 420–421.

Ulrich, R.S. (1991), 'Effects of Interior Design on Wellness; Theory and Recent Scientific Research', *Journal of Health Care Interior Design*.

Ulrich, R.S., and Simons, R.F. (April 1986), 'Recovery from stress during exposure to everyday outdoor environments', *Proceedings of the Seventeenth Annual Conference of the Environmental Design Research Association*.

Internet

Book, J. (1995), US Garden Design, *Bali High,* viewed 3 September 2006, www.ptwijaya.com/Media/garden-design.html

Dunn, E. (2006), 'Controversial and classic up for action', Arts Reviews, *Sydney Morning Herald*, viewed 25 August, http://www.smh.com.au/news/arts/aussie-art-for-sale/2006/08/24/1w012675800.html

Kiracofe, J.B. (1995), 'Cultural Integration and Architectural Fusion as a Strategy for Survival: the Iconographic Use of Disk Frieze ornament in Pre-Columbian and Early-Colonial Buildings', presented to a conference of the Inter-American Institute for Advanced Studies in Cultural history, http://www.interamericaninstitute.org/vpi-1995-conference.

Olsen, M. (1999), *Mexico: Images of Dry Tropical Habitat*, viewed 21 September 2006, http://www.mobot.org/gradstudents/olson/mexicolandscapes.html

Shaw, E., with assistance from Favell, I. (2006), *Bali,* viewed 1 September 2006, http://en.wikipedia.org/wiki/Bali

Taylor, L. (1997), 'Plumeria perfect for Oahu', Ever Green, *Honolulu Star-Bulletin*, Honolulu, http://starbulletin.com/97/09/09/features/evergreen.html

http://www.balilife.com/arts/dance/dancel.html

http://www.indo.com/culture/dance_music.html

Email

Wijaya, M. (2006), Frangipanis are the ballerinas, Easy to move at almost any size, 18 September to Linda Ross.

Olson, M. (2006), *Plumeria request,* 22 September to Linda Ross.

Crull, M. (2006), *FW: Plumeria request*, 23 September to Linda Ross.

OPPOSITE: Unknown cultivar, Sydney, Australia.

Thank You

The authors wish to sincerely thank the following people:

Mr Michael Ferrero, Former Curator, Nong Nooch Tropical Botanical Garden, Thailand for whom special thanks is given for reading out draft, his helpful suggestions and enthusiasm for the work.

Dr Richard Criley, Professor of Horticulture, University of Hawai'i.

Mr Leland Miyano, landscape designer, plant collector, artist, author, environmentalist and truly inspirational gardener on Oahu, Hawai'i.

Mr David Orr, Botanical Program Co-ordinator, Waimea Valley Audubon Centre, O'ahu, Hawai'i

Mrs Raynel Foster, plumeria grower, O'ahu, Hawai'i.

Mr James Mason, plumeria enthusiast and photographer, Honolulu, Hawai'i.

Mr Fuzzy Moody, plumeria enthusiast and talented gardener, Honolulu, Hawai'i.

Naomi Hoffman, Botanist, Honolulu Botanical Gardens, Hawai'i.

Mr Jim Little, plumeria enthusiast, breeder and author/photographer, O'ahu, Hawai'i.

Mr Donald Herron, President, photographic collector and founder of the Plumeria Society, Florida, USA.

Mike 'DJ' Earnshaw, frangipani specialist, DJ's Way Nursery, Tweed Heads, Australia.

Made Wijaya, landscape designer, Bali.

Ross McKinnon, Mt Coot-tha Botanic Gardens, Brisbane, Australia.

Kym West, frangipani enthusiast, Queensland, Australia.

Don Ellison, frangipani enthusiast and tour operator, Queensland, Australia.

Barbara Simmons, artist, USA.

Mary Jane Crull, South Texas Botanical Garden and Nature Centre

OPPOSITE: Relax with this peaceful tropical garden.

OPPOSITE: 'Celadine'.

Mark Olson, botanist specialising in Dry Tropical Habitats, Missouri Botanical Garden and Washington University in St Louis.

Dr. Dorothy Gibson-Wilde, historian, Townsville, Australia.

Mr Steven Prowse, Sacred Garden Frangipanis, Mount Garnet, Far North Queensland, Australia.

Mr Vince Winkel, former Parks, Curator Flecker Botanic Gardens, Cairns, Australia.

Mr Tom Wyatt, former council forman, Townsville, Australia.

Megan Martin and staff at Historic Houses Trust Caroline Simpson Collection, Sydney, Australia.

Mr. Brendan Lewis, landscaper, Avoca, Australia.

Luca Invernizzi Tettoni, photographer, Singapore.

Notebook Magazine, Australia.

Jada Bennett, floral stylist, Sydney, Australia.

Margaret Cory Garden Designs, Sydney, Australia.

Noelene Hambly, who kindly made the frangipane tart, Sydney, Australia.

Mauri Maunsell, Brisbane, Australia.

Lindsey Gerchow and Yves Daniel, Buderim Landscapes, Buderim, Queensland, Australia.

Kim Packman, frangipani enthusiast, Tweed Heads, Australia.

The Garden Clinic, Sydney, Australia.

Gardens and Garden Designers

Pg 6: Bob Dodds, Roma Street Parkland, Brisbane, Qld.

Pg 12: The garden of Claudia Nevell, Landscape Designer, Coffs Harbour, NSW.

Pg 14: The garden of Mr & Mrs King, Avoca, NSW, designed by Brendan Lewis, Avoca, NSW.

Pg 15: The garden of Jane Rogers, Sydney, New South Wales, designed by Hugh Main, Spirit Level Design.

Pg 21: 'Trees and Shrubs' manuscript albums British, c 1802-04 Volume 1 (detail from folio 20).

Pg 36: Vaucluse, NSW. Designed by Hugh Main, Spirit Level Design.

Pg 37: The garden of Mr and Mrs Fletcher, Sydney, New South Wales, designed by Hugh Main from Spirit Level Design.

Pg 39: The garden of Mr M. Robison, Goonengerry, New South Wales, designed by Tim Hays Design, Burringbar, New South Wales.

Pg 79: The garden of Mr and Mrs O'Keefe, Woody Point, Queensland. Designed by Phillip O'Malley Garden Design.

Pg 100: The garden of Brendan and Emma Clark, Sunshine Coast Frangipani Farm, Diddilibah, Queensland.

Pg 131: The garden of Mr M Robison, Goonengerry, New South Wales, designed by Tim Hays Garden Design, Burringbar, New South Wales.

Pg 132: The garden of Robin Powell, Sydney, Australia.

Pg 136: The garden of Mr and Mrs Dalziel, Queensland.

Pg 138: Oceanic Imports, Doonan, Queensland.

Pg 139: Nusa Dua Beach Hotel, Bali.

Pg 140: Nusa Dua Beach Hotel, Bali.

OPPOSITE: 'Celadine', Sydney, Australia.

OPPOSITE: Unknown cultivar, Sydney, Australia.

Pg 141: Courtyard designed by Glen Murcutt, Australian architect.

Pg 145: Prana Villas, Seminyak, Bali.

Pg 149: The garden of Lorna Rose, Sydney, Australia.

Pg 162: Bill Bensley Residence, Bangkok, Thailand

Pg 166: The garden of Leland Miyano, Oahu, Hawai'i.

Pg 174: Petchaburi, Khao Wang, Thailand.

Pg 182: Matrimandir Gardens, India.

Pg 188: The flowers of Jada Bennett, floral stylist, Sydney.

Pg 191: The wedding chapel at Tirtha Uluwatu, Uluwatu, Bali.

Pg 214: The garden of Neville Sloss and Glauber Luz, 'Larapinta', Teven, NSW.

Photographers

We'd like to thank the following photographers for contributing the following images:

Linda Ross: Pg 79 (below), Pg 90, Pg 93, Pg 101, Pg 102, Pg 123, Pg 124, Pg 139, Pg 140, Pg 145, Pg 153 (below), Pg 177.

Luca Tettoni Invernezzi: Pg 32, Pg 128/129, Pg 157, Pg 162, Pg 174, Pg 177 (top), Pg 189.

Michael 'DJ' Earnshaw from DJ's Way: Pg 50 (below), Pg 82, Pg 106 (below), Pg 150, Pg 182.

Anton van der Schans: Pg 26, Pg 28, Pg 65, Pg 153 top, Pg 172 (top).

Steve Prowse from Sacred Garden Frangipani: Pg 118.

Nigel and Kym West, Gold Coast: Pg 65, Pg 120/121.

Tirtha Uluwatu, Uluwatu, Bali: Pg 191.

Scott Hawkins, Sydney: Pg 91.

John Stowar: Pg 72.

Peter Hyatt: Pg 141.

Trevor Cochrane: Pg 73.

Andrew O'Sullivan: Pg 65, Pg 88.

Notebook Magazine: Pg 132, Pg 188.

Barbara Simmons: Pg 195.

Peter Whitehead: Pg 178.

OPPOSITE: 'Black Red', Tweed Heads, Australia.